A Sales Mindset

How To Prepare For Success

Jonathan Frost

First published 2017 by Discovery Coaching

Copyright © Jonathan Frost

ISBN: 1547027800
ISBN-13: 978-1547027804

Also by Jonathan Frost

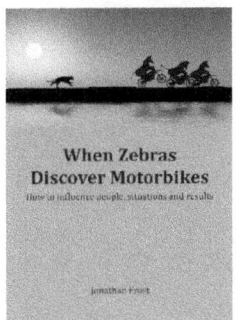

When Zebras Discover Motorbikes

Life in the Serengeti changes significantly when the zebras discover motorbikes. The 'natural order' that the lions enjoy is changed. The 'zebra analogy' talks about change at work and draws your attention to the typical reactions that people have. This book has a practical approach and provides managers with a wide range of tips, hints and techniques to engage with and thrive on organisational change. It has an engaging 'coaching' approach that provokes you to think deeper, see things differently and do different things.

Available on Amazon

Also by Jonathan Frost

Meetings That Make A Difference

Meetings certainly matter! They enable some helpful discussions, vital debate and wise decision making. This book provides you with a wide range of tips, hints and techniques that you can use to make sure that your meetings make a difference. It includes...

The 7 practices of good meeting facilitators
10 Traps to avoid
How to influence group dynamics
7 Powerful meeting tactics
A 24-point coaching checklist

Available on Amazon

CONTENTS

About the author | 6

Introduction | 7

1 What is Selling? | 13

2 What is Sales Management? | 27

3 A Sales Mindset | 35

4 An Enterprising Mindset | 55
YOU plc

5 A Value-Add Mindset | 79

6 An Engaged Mindset | 95

7 A Practical Mindset | 109

8 A Summary of the Tips, Hints and | 149
Techniques

ABOUT THE AUTHOR

Jonathan Frost is the Managing Director and Founder of Discovery Coaching Limited. Working across Europe he has assisted hundreds of sales professionals, sales managers and sales directors over the last 19 years. He consults for organisations, develops sales training programmes, implements workshops and provides 1:1 coaching.

He has a unique ability to provoke thought and trigger helpful discoveries. His focus is on enabling participants to discover the practical tips, hints and techniques that are relevant to their everyday business life. Jonathan developed the coaching methodology known as 'Discovery Coaching' and this proven approach helps individuals to develop their business approach and maximise their performance. He is an inspirational coach who motivates individuals to exceed their goals.

Jonathan has extensive experience working with Sales Professionals at all levels in many different organisations; from small enterprises right through to large multinationals.

INTRODUCTION

This book is for those who spend their working life influencing people. It is for those engaged in selling products, services, ideas or opportunities – which is most of us when you think about it. If your job involves persuading people, you will discover some helpful approaches and techniques that you can apply immediately.

If you engage in the 'coaching questions' at the end of each chapter the thought processes will help you to discover better ways of doing things. I call them 'thought-provokers' as they trigger you to think much more deeply about the subject than you might otherwise do. The suggested 'discovery activities' present you with an opportunity to apply the learning and make sure that the content is helpful and directly relevant to your particular working world. It is the engagement with the thought-provokers that will convert your reading from a theoretical exercise into a powerful and directly relevant learning experience. It is your ability to convert day-to-day activities into learning experiences that will enable you to make significant improvements to your expertise.

A Sales Mindset

In what way is this book different from the multitude of other books on selling that are available to you? There are two significant differences and these can enable you to gain a real competitive advantage over those who are not engaged in this type of thinking.

Firstly it is all about a *Sales Mindset*. A mindset is a consistent approach or way of thinking. It is an established set of attitudes or outlooks that drive your choices and behaviours. Right now you have a particular sales mindset; it is unique to you and is made up of the many influences and influencers in your working life. This includes people you admire, people you dislike and the situations that have engaged or challenged you. It also includes the customers that have impacted you, the successes you have enjoyed and the failures you have learned from. An important contributor is also the training and development activities you have engaged in. Your sales mindset is not accidental; it is a logical result of your experiences to date and it is definitely impacting your performance and the quality of your working life. It needs neither your awareness nor your permission to influence you and this means that it is worth carefully thinking about.
It is wise to see your own personal mindset as being very much 'work in progress; it helps you to evolve your working environment and context. This book is going to help you to understand it; it will also enable you to helpfully question and improve it.

Secondly, this book is different because it is going to provide you with the tips and techniques to coach yourself and others to sell better. Your willingness and ability to coach yourself will provide you with a rapid increase in enthusiasm, energy and capability; it will noticeably improve your performance. As you engage in discovering better ways to approach things and do things, you will accelerate your personal development and naturally convert day-to-day work into powerful learning experiences. One of the cruellest myths that society teaches people about 'betterment' is the phrase, 'practice makes perfect'. Practice does not make perfection; it simply ensures consistency. I am reminded of the hours I spent at a golf driving range hitting ball after ball and getting so frustrated that I was not making any marked improvement in my game. Basically I was under the illusion that just because I did more and more of a thing I would somehow become better at it. I became very efficient at applying poor techniques and rather than improve my game I 'locked-in' bad habits. If you keep practicing unhelpful ways at doing things then you simply become very efficient and consistent at these unhelpful ways. In this situation efficiency masquerades as effectiveness because there is no introduction of new thinking, techniques or processes.

This is why the coaching element is so important to your personal improvement; you need to provoke yourself to discover new outlooks and approaches that trigger you to helpfully change your ways of working. This allows you to discover the techniques, activities and processes that work much better for you. Engage with the coaching questions, checklists and other thought provoking processes that accompany every chapter; use them to trigger a change in the way that you think. The time that you spend pondering over them is valuable time that you are spending 'reconfiguring' your sales mindset.

If you set out to coach others to apply the principles, tips and techniques…you will accelerate your own learning even faster! Consider the following analogy that proves this point.

Imagine for a minute that you are a medical student learning all about eye surgery. You have been asked to observe at an operation so that you can see the process and learn from the experience. You read up about it and then you watch a master at work. It is an intense and very helpful learning experience; you have seen what the 'good' do and gained practical insight.

Imagine that you are then asked to actually perform that same operation yourself on a patient. Your level of engagement dramatically increases. Your studying now takes on a new relevance and your 'experience' of the actual operation is so much deeper and richer than simply watching it. You learn much from watching and reading about things; you learn much more however from actually doing it and having your performance observed and evaluated.

You are then asked, in this same analogy, to teach a group of students about this very same surgical procedure. By watching and then actually carrying out the operation you have learned much and have much to pass on. When you start teaching others however you realise the need for more in-depth knowledge and the need to carefully and logically explain principles, practices and procedures. Doing this provides you with an even richer overall learning experience; it helps you because it reinforces all the things that have to take place and it ensures that you thoroughly understand everything.

So we see that watching others do things (or reading about them), actually doing things yourself and then teaching others to do them provides a thorough and robust learning experience. Doing all three is a significantly smarter approach than just doing one of them. This can be explained as different levels of learning.

Level 1 learning – Observing others
Level 2 learning – Doing it yourself
Level 3 learning – Coaching others

That is why I am advising you to read the book, do the things in it…and then coach others to do it as well. Use the tips, hints, checklists and coaching questions to coach others – it will really help you!

Jonathan Frost

1

WHAT IS SELLING?

How do you personally define 'Selling?'

This is not a rhetorical question, I am actually asking you to define the concept of selling. If you had to write up a dictionary definition, what would you say? When asked to do this many people start talking about the different stages of selling or what the selling process looks like: but that does not answer the question. Most people find this a tricky exercise and I would strongly urge you to put the book down for a few minutes, take up a pencil and some paper and craft a definition. Ideally I am looking for just one coherent sentence that captures it all. It has been said that if you cannot explain something simply...then you do not understand it. I like this thinking; as sales professionals it should be easy for us to define 'selling' but unfortunately the concept is something that we have not spent much time thinking about. We think about what we do without realising that this is actually driven by our internal definitions and understandings. Let me explain why this 'defining things' is so important...

The above question is an important one for you; your personal understanding of the subject greatly shapes your approach and activities. It is undoubtedly the single biggest influencer on your sales mindset and on your success. It triggers you to see things in a certain way and from a specific perspective. It provokes you to feel that some activities are more important than others and that some have better value than others. It obviously makes sense therefore to validate and sense-check your current perception. Do not look for what you agree with or disagree with when you read this chapter, don't just tick off the things you already knew; spend your time trying to enrich your understanding and working context. Look for discoveries as opposed to confirmation. Seek out areas that provoke discomfort rather than those that support your comfort zone. Use this as an opportunity to improve and drive your performance.

Think on this question – 'How can you enrich your personal definition in order to add value to your outlook and self-coaching?'

Typically 'selling' is understood to have taken place when something is exchanged for money. When we go to the shops; we hand over our money and in exchange we get to keep the items that are in our basket. Strictly speaking each of these items has been sold to us; they were attractively displayed, we were tempted and we then made a decision to exchange our money for them. Whilst no human interaction took place when the sale was made it was still very much a case of others consciously encouraging and influencing you to buy. These people were not present but their work was and it is their work (visual merchandising, positioning, signs, package design etc.) that directly influenced you. Perhaps you think that human interaction did in fact take place during the sale - at the till point when money exchanged hands. I would suggest that this was simply the carrying out of the transaction and this took place only after the decision to buy was made. It finalised the sale, it did not encourage you to buy.

The selling process can be non-verbal; it does not require a human interaction. It is often enhanced by human interaction however.

This is important to you and it should influence your tactics. Whatever your product, most times, the sales process has commenced before your personal interaction; the more influence you can have over this the easier it will be for you. The better that you understand these 'silent' influences on your customers the easier it will be to understand their perspective and priming. This applies just as much whether you are selling a physical product, a service or an idea.

Let's use a different commercial situation that is common to all of us i.e. our electricity supply to our homes. It can be said that our Utility 'sells' electricity to us every month, we use it and they bill us regularly. As long as we pay our bills they keep supplying the power. Strictly speaking perhaps we are being sold electricity every month but in reality selling is not taking place. Yes we are handing over money and they are providing something in exchange for it however this is simply a repeated transaction that has resulted from selling that took place previously. There is no persuasion or encouragement involved in this interaction and that is why it is not selling; an agreement is simply being fulfilled. Some time earlier the utility company advertised their services, engaged you in discussions and made a persuasive proposition for you to choose their package. You considered this, weighed up the options and made a choice. In this process you made a binding decision to commit to this package – and that was when the sale was made. That was the sales process. On a monthly basis the Utility is simply 'fulfilling' what has been already sold.

The distinction between 'fulfilment' and 'selling' is an important one for the professional salesperson because if a company has agreed to 100 widgets being delivered each month, you are not in fact selling that amount each month; you are just fulfilling it. If they are taking only 80 widgets and you need to remedy this then you are then engaged in discussion about compliance to the agreement; this is not selling and you should have a very different approach. *You would not want to use up your valuable sales resources such as your time, promotions or incentives in re-selling what has already been bought.* Re-selling what has already been sold is one of the bigger traps that you need to avoid. If you engage in it you actually legitimise the need for it because you have suddenly accepted that the previous selling and decision is now nullified. You then end up using your 'sweeteners' and negotiating points twice for the same sale. You should rather use these 'sales enablers' for new business, different business or extra business.

A definition of 'selling'

So lets come back to that activity that I prompted you to engage in at the beginning of the chapter. I asked you to define what the word 'selling' actually means. Typically definitions are all about exchanging goods for money or convincing people to buy. This is good and true however it is useful to add more to it; so I have provided a definition below.

Selling is the process of persuading people to make decisions and take actions.

This is an easy to remember definition that you should memorise and take to heart. We see that there are four simple but highly important elements; it is the combination of them, the rich blend, that converts an interaction into a productive sales interaction. The elements are...

1. Process
2. Persuasion
3. Decision Making
4. Specific Action

Process. Essentially a process is a series of interconnected and interdependent steps that will result in a consistent result. This is very important to you; it is how you consistently get good results through inspiration and not perspiration. It allows you to focus on bigger issues and opportunities because you do not have to think hard about each step along the way. If you break down activities into their logical and sequential steps then you can recognise your strengths and weaknesses for each one and you can choose to build up your mastery. If you do not identify the core elements of a process then it is hard to know what to improve. You may be getting good results but not know why you are being successful. You don't know what is triggering the good outcomes and that means you cannot influence them. In the business of selling, the stages or steps are very often interdependent i.e. they rely on each other for progress. It is little use being brilliant at just some of them because the others may just cut off your progress. If you are a skilled 'closer' but you find 'active listening' difficult then you may not get the chance to excel at closing because you have lost your way in the interaction before you got the opportunity.

Persuasion. This is the art of developing and presenting a reasoned argument in a way that is attractive, compelling and convincing. It is attractive because it demonstrates some clear advantages and benefits that can be gained from this proposal. It is compelling because it arrests the attention of the other person; it is impactful and consumes their attention and focus. It is convincing because the challenges or objections to it have been considered and overcome; the reasons why it will work have been enthusiastically explained. This is all about getting the other person to see things differently, to see them the way you do and to be convinced that this is indeed a better way.

I would suggest that without persuasion there is no selling. Simply informing a customer of the 'facts' is not enough. Sterile facts seldom trigger passionate responses. I have people say to me that 'selling is simply presenting the data in a way that the customer can see the benefits'. Whilst I know what they mean and their thinking is not totally wrong, I would have to say that it is flawed! Influential salespeople know that customers can see the benefits; but they still want the opportunity to confirm those benefits, to link them together and to show them even more. They want to highlight and reinforce those benefits; to ensure that they have maximum impact. Good salespeople want to get across the 'persuasive story' that has impact. This is being persuasive as opposed to just being communicative. You want customers to 'see' and 'feel' what you are saying rather than just intellectually calculate the benefits that could accrue. This might be about persuading the other person to see the benefits of your service and so be attracted to them. It might be persuading them to act now rather than later i.e. decide today rather than 'think about it'. It might even be persuading them to see your business as the first choice when they are in the market for your products. Different customers are motivated by different things and for some the logical argument is compelling and yet for others the passionate emotional argument creates the point of persuasion.

Decision-making. Selling always involves decisions. This might be to purchase a product, accept a concept or agree to your proposition. It is an active choice. Essentially a decision is the selection of one option from a range of choices. It is a binding choice; it is an undertaking, obligation or promise that is not intended to be broken. When you feel you have made a sale, sense check the customers decision against these factors. Does the customer see their decision as final? Do they see their choice as helpfully binding?

When your customer has decided to trial your product, buy a range or appoint you as the sole provider of products; they have made a binding choice. There is a difference between a 'decision in principle' and a 'binding decision'. The difference is that the first one is not actually a decision; it is a half commitment with a pre-prepared exit route! It is important to recognise that a sales decision is quite binary i.e. there are only two parts to it. Essentially it is all about 'yes' or 'no' in a selling context. When someone says "maybe' or "I'll think about it" or "We are waiting for new budgets to be finalised" they are actually saying 'no'. This could be perfectly reasonable and it does not reflect failure and should not be seen as such. Neither should it be seen as success however because the third option of 'maybe' is not really a third option; it is just a different way of saying 'no'. This is not just a point of semantics; if you have a 'no' and you see it as a weak 'yes' then it will unhelpfully influence your tactics and approach. Misreading the situation isolates you from opportunities to persuade and convert the decision.

Specific Action. This is the specific activity that will take place, as a result of the decision. It is a vital component of selling because it represents the rationale for doing it all in the first place. You want your customer to do something. This might be about providing an order number or signing a contract. Hopefully it involves exchanging their money for your products, services, ideas, intellectual property or assets. It is absolutely essential that you have clarity about what you want your customer to decide to do when you enter into a sales interaction; you need to have clarity about this in advance so that your insight and intentions can helpfully influence your tactics.

Wise and strong selling is never a fishing activity. You don't just throw a number of fishing lines overboard with a bit of bait and wait to see what 'bites'. That might work for professional fishermen but it does not reflect professional salesmanship! You need to know what actions your customer needs to take in order to progress the sales opportunity or decision. That is one of the reasons that you would work hard to understand their business model, ways of working and operating constraints.

So we see that selling has four distinct elements to it which can be summarised as... "The process of persuading people to make decisions and take actions".

This is how, for the purposes of this book, we define selling. Essentially this means convincing people to act. It is about triggering choices and provoking decisions. In the retail example mentioned a number of pages ago the display was set out to attract your attention and present the products in an attractive way; with the intention of making you buy. The Utility engaged with you and presented a persuasive argument to provoke your decision to use their services; they then wanted you to take the specific action of signing a long-term contract.

It would not have been a successful sale, even if you had stood on top of the Eiffel Tower shouting at the top of your voice how determined you were to change your Utility...if you had not signed the contract as well!

Selling is not just about persuading people to change their minds and *want* to take action; it is about convincing them to actually take that action. The examples that I have provided above are admittedly very simplistic; they are just a way to extract and demonstrate the four key elements.

The key elements still apply in more complex sales situations; they simply stretch out over a much longer period of time. Imagine that you are a sales professional engaged in selling an executive jet to a corporation. This is going to take some time. Due to the high cost of the product, the 'persuasion' element must reach out to many different people, probably in many different locations; all of them will have different needs and requirements. A multitude of different arguments must persuade a multitude of people that this is the right solution for this corporation. The decision making process will therefore have many different 'gates' or stages to go through. These look at the proposition from different perspectives and again this is going to involve different people, stakeholder groups and levels of authority. Each of these stages need decisions to be approved and actions to be taken as a result. This is showing the complexity of this particular sales process and it demonstrates that provoking some key people in the organisation to 'want a jet' is just not going to be enough. Professional salespeople need to have insight, influence and credibility to influence the whole of the sales process. We will talk more of this in later chapters but it proves the need for you to have a very wide 'sphere of influence' so that you can be influential in all areas.

In most organisations this process of persuasion,

decision-making and action-taking affect every single activity and almost every employee. Individuals need to persuade others; groups need to persuade divisions; key managers have to persuade the board to spend money – internally the process goes on continuously and we have not even got to the external selling activities yet! It is for this reason that the adoption of a 'persuasive mindset' or a 'sales mindset' is not just for the external sales team. Ideas, concepts and plans have to be sold – not just products.

It is self evident that every influential person in every organisation needs to sell ideas and choices. They need to persuade other people and organisations to 'buy into' concepts and decisions. This is actually how they get to be influential – people and groups are persuaded by them. This is not just for the sales division but it is especially for them.

The deeper and richer that you engage with these key elements of selling the more opportunities you will see to further develop your capability and results. One of the ways of doing this is to engage in the coaching questions on the following page.

Coaching Questions

Invest some time in your expertise and capability to consider these questions. I would strongly recommend that you don't just read them for understanding but rather that you put some time aside and role play an interview in your mind. Imagine you are being interviewed by journalist from a trade magazine; Sales Professional Magazine is interviewing you and these are the questions that they are asking…

How persuasive are you?

If your customers accused you of being 'highly persuasive' – what examples or recent evidence would they present in order to prove their case? What could you do to be even more persuasive?

Do you consciously plan compelling and highly persuasive sales presentations?

If you are selling a worldwide brand it is very easy to rely on the product's history and reputation to be persuasive. Do you still have the passion to create a compelling and convincing sales pitch for products that you have been selling a long time, to long-standing customers?

In the last 6 months, what is the presentation or sales interaction that you would like to be most remembered for?

What do your customers find compelling and convincing?

What sparks their interest and consumes their focus and attention? What are the key areas that your customers need convincing in? What are the areas that they are most 'unsold' about?

What do you do to test that your 'points of persuasion' are still valid and strong?

Who can you speak to? Who would be honest? What would you ask them?

Do you fully understand your customer's decision-making process?

We noted that the larger organisations have 'gate' processes that they must go through to progress the bigger purchases. This ensures that all the relevant issues are covered and the appropriate people are engaged. Do you understand all the key elements and different key stakeholders that your customers have to consider? Can you fully describe the 'working context' of the person that you are selling to?

Do you fully understand the levels of decision-making authority of the person that you are selling to?
We will discover later on in this book that there are many different roles that contribute to the buying process. Are you being realistic about what you can expect from this meeting? Are you talking to the right person?

Are you driven by compelling goals or just aspirations?
Whilst this is a subject that will be covered in depth later on, it is well worth considering at this early stage. Do you have very specific goals that you want to achieve for your sales interactions? Whilst you will always strive to be flexible and agile in the meeting, it is important to have specific end goals that you want to achieve. 'To sell as much as possible' is not a goal; it is simply an aspiration or an intention.. 'To persuade them to increase the monthly order to 150 widgets' is a goal!

Suggested Activities

a.   Develop a table that records the different stages of your customer's buying process. Spend some time on this to capture the complexities.

b.   Note the key stages. What has to happen at each stage before it goes on to the next stage? By doing this you record a 'critical path analysis' of the decision. You can use this information to carefully consider what events, situations and processes that you need to influence.

c.   Note the people who are key to each stage.

d.   Assess your level of influence and relationship. Do you understand their drivers, issues and opportunities? Do you know their aspirations, vision and goals? Do you know what the 'indicators of success' are for their own role? How could you help them to look good in their organisations?

The purpose of this chapter was to clarify what we mean by selling and to introduce the three key elements.

2

WHAT IS SALES MANAGEMENT?

In the previous chapter we talked about the importance to your sales mindset of a clear and full definition of what selling actually is. In this chapter we briefly move onto the important topic of sales management.

The title is a very relevant question for all involved in the sales process, whether you are a sales person, sales manager or sales director. Please don't skip this chapter just because this is not your job title - *because it is still very much your role.* The word 'Manager' has become a generic term for someone who is 'in charge' or 'responsible for' and we have to dig a bit deeper than that if we want to discover a more helpful meaning that is rich and has practical usefulness. A Sales Manager is one who plans, organises, controls and coordinates all the activities within the business that directly relate to sales. They lead, control and administer the selling process that their business engages in. It is a wide role that requires broad business experience and an ability to helpfully interact with people. It is an influential role that impacts the whole organisation.

A major focus of that role however is to directly manage the sales team. This has to go beyond simply organizing their 'pay and rations', it must extend to influencing their outlook and approach, expanding their capability and providing helpful resources.

It is my view that in times of high workload, demanding targets and tight budgets it is this last part of the role (people leadership and development) that has generally been allowed to dissipate and fade away in many organisations. Very often it is not a measureable part of the Sales Manager role so this unhelpful change can go unnoticed. Monthly reports seldom include hours spent coaching sales people; they often don't list continued professional development activities. Reporting processes do not focus on or capture the inspirational sales meetings, or telephone coaching. The activities that motivate and encourage the sales team are often not reported on whilst administration practices, reports and sales metrics certainly are. The work sales managers do in the unblocking of internal 'sales-prevention' activities within the business is often under appreciated and even hindered. There will be a focus on the hard metrics of what has happened without a corresponding element of what has taken place to create capability and build expertise.

Perhaps the answer is to differentiate between management activities and leadership activities. Whilst management is all about the controlling, organizing and coordinating – the leadership activities are all about influencing people and situations in order to achieve outstanding results. The leadership element involves setting a clear direction and establishing a strategy for individuals to follow. It involves inspiring people to see what can be achieved and giving them the confidence and ability to stretch their performance. I firmly believe that generally this element of Sales Management has definitely taken a back seat as organisations become more complex. As more and more data becomes available, more is expected and Sales Managers are required to spend more and more time on it. As organisational structures become leaner workloads pass on to Sales Managers and they spend more time ensuring that internal processes are functioning correctly than ensuring that 'points of customer interaction' are functioning optimally.

What does all the above mean to you if you are not a Sales Manager? Actually it means a lot because that personal development element of that role cascades to you. The setting of direction, management of focus, analysis of performance and development of capability – becomes your role for you! The successful professional sales person is now largely self-managing and this has to extend far beyond just discipline, work ethic and time management. It must extend to areas such as being self-motivated, engaging in self-coaching and being self-directed. You need to have the *mindset* that makes you a quick learner with the agility to change outlooks and 'ways of working' in an instant. The ability to do this expands your expertise and capability; it also significantly increases your 'market value' because you are able to win better results. It is probably a system that favours the self-motivated, but then again doesn't everything?

The successful sales person is now largely self-managing.

This assertion presents itself to you as either a disappointing threat or a wonderful opportunity. It is a threat if you feel that you have a 'right' to expect your organisation to develop your expertise and invest in your future. I must point out that this is not a right as such and it probably never was; in the past however it was certainly a common and valid expectation. Of course there are organisations out there who are brilliant examples of proactive leadership and they rightly have accolades for the ways that they develop and invest in people. Such organisations win awards for being the 'best employers' and they draw talent to themselves because of this. Think about this though; if you can get an award for being a great employer, then there must be an awful lot of companies out there who are not 'great employers', otherwise they would not be giving awards for it! You should not necessarily think harshly about your employer if they don't do it the way that the very best large organisations do it because there has, in my view, been a cultural shift. It is not that companies don't value their people, it is simply that they expect them to be much more self-managing. Your development could be your USP (unique sales proposition) or it could be your Achilles heel (your point of vulnerability) – the choice is actually yours.

This could be a great opportunity for you! Imagine, if you will, what it must be like to be crouched down at the start of a 110m hurdles race. It is the Olympics and the huge audience grow quiet for the start. You look forward and you see a set of ten hurdles in front of you. How do you see them? Are they bits of annoying wood in your way as you run as fast as you can; are they ten opportunities for you to be better than the people on either side of you? If you are good at setting your pace; you can meet each hurdle at just the right time so that you can skim over it without breaking your stride…then you will see the hurdle as an opportunity. You will see it as an opportunity to differentiate yourself from the others; you will see each hurdle as an opportunity to excel.

Everyone in the race has the same challenge and if they are not so skilled at hurdles then they can become 10 individual threats to success. This is how it is for you in terms of being self-motivated and being able to be self-learning. Just see that requirement as being a part of the race now. The 110m hurdler is not outraged at these things in her way, she sees them as a part of the game and uses each one of them to gain some competitive advantage.

Sales Management has become more of an 'activity' than a job title.

Perhaps Sales *Self-Management* would be a better title? If you want to become an expert at inspiring, motivating and developing people – why not start with yourself! This is good for your current performance and it is also good for your career development. Proving that you can engage in all areas of the selling process and be influential in making it better will greatly enhance your career prospects. See yourself as your first employee to manage and your situation as the first situation to helpfully change.

The rest of this book will give you some valuable

tips, techniques and process to help you with your self-coaching and self-management. The coaching questions below will kick-start this discovery process if you allow them to.

Coaching Questions

These 'thought-provokers' relate to the concept of self-management.

In the last 12 months, how much of your own money have you spent on developing your expertise?
This might be about books that you have bought, podcasts you have downloaded or magazines that you have subscribed to. Does the 'investment' that you have made reflect the actions of an ambitious, successful and high-potential sales professional? Do not feel bad about your answer if it is not a strong investment…for most people this is a bit of a 'wake-up' point.

Have you identified areas in which you could be even better at your role?
This might be about developing new skills, gaining new knowledge, having new experiences or creating better outlooks. It is my experience that you only notice these opportunities if you look for them. You need a structured process to 'self-evaluate' and this is provided later in the book.

What is your view about the fact that you need to be quite 'self managing'?
Do you currently see this as an opportunity or a threat to your performance? Right now is this

something that gives you a competitive advantage over others...or does it give them an advantage over you?

Suggested Activities

Later in this book you will find a 40-point self-assessment checklist. Select a week in the near future which you designate as an 'introspection week'. Use this time to objectively question all that you do and why you do it. Use the self-assessment questionnaire as a part of this week's activity. More to follow later.

Jonathan Frost

3

A SALES MINDSET

I briefly explained the 'Mindset' concept in the introduction. It is a consistent approach or way of thinking. Actually it is quite self explanatory, your mind is 'set' in the way it sees, perceives and interprets things. This means that your approach to things will be consistent and that you are not overwhelmed by every single possibility when you are confronted with a situation or event. You see it and approach it according to your 'set' patterns.

A mindset is to the mind what sunglasses are to the eyes i.e. a filter that changes the appearance of everything. It does not change the things themselves, just how they look to you personally. Remember that nobody else benefits from your sunglasses; they only change the way that things look to you. So it is with your mindset; it makes sense of things and provides you with context…but it may well be different for others.

Your mindset is your established set of attitudes or outlooks that drive your choices and behaviours. Right now you have a particular sales mindset; it is unique to you and is made up of the many influences and influencers in your working life. This includes people you have worked with, worked for and competed against. It is influenced by the people and situations in your current working world and from your past. This obviously also includes the customers that have impacted you, the successes you have enjoyed and the failures you have learned from. An important contributor is also the training and development activities you have engaged in.

Your sales mindset is not accidental; it is a logical result of your experiences to date and how you have chosen to understand and interpret them. It is definitely impacting your performance as well as the quality of your working life; as said earlier, it needs neither your awareness nor your permission to influence you. All of this tells you that it is something that is worth carefully thinking about. This book is going to help you to understand it; it will also enable you to helpfully question and improve it.

Why do you have a mindset?

Imagine if you did not have one and you needed to thoroughly think through absolutely everything you do! Every single task would be a major undertaking that would be time consuming, exhausting and frustrating. Let's apply this to an example to see how impractical this is; you decide to drive from your home to the local shopping centre that is 10 miles away. First of all you have to get a map out and work out all of the different routes that could take you there (there is no 'usual' route). You have to establish a values based list of criteria for choosing which of the 7 possible routes you could take. Each of these criteria has to be considered in depth to analyse their true worth and to understand the consistency and stability of the benefits that they bring. You then might rank them hierarchically so that they can be compared to others. Of course you need to validate the benefits of each of the criteria and this causes you another problem. You realise that you had better check the weather forecasts and the road works notices to see if they will impact your journey. This means that you need to research which weather forecaster has the best accuracy...by this time you are feeling malnourished and you phone for a take-away pizza!

This is why you have a mindset. You have an established way of thinking that has 'locked in' your preferred 'ways of working'; it captures your logic, values and preferences and uses them as drivers for your decisions and actions. It means that your actions are regulated and prompted by your values. It enables your thoughts, decisions and approaches to be consistent and in accordance to your preferred way of doing things. It helps you to act both promptly and wisely to challenges and opportunities. In the silly example above you would simply just take your 'usual' route and spend your precious cognitive capability on other things.

This is a powerful ability that saves you a lot of time because it is so much more efficient; it also therefore saves you a great deal of mental energy that you can put to better use. By having this established 'operating system' that does not need everything to be questioned you can put your considerable focus, attention and intelligence to things that can make a real difference to you and your organisation. You can take on the significant challenges and convert them into opportunities and this is particularly important for selling and business development. *The smooth running of your mindset can free up 'mental bandwidth' that can allow you to have superior alertness and awareness.* This is ideal for you because you need to listen and watch very carefully in sales situations.

A good analogy of a mindset is an 'autopilot' in an aircraft. Contrary to popular belief the autopilot does not actually fly the plane – the pilot flies it using the autopilot as an 'automation tool'. The pilot is always in charge but hands over some of the more mundane tasks to a computer. It means he does not have to be literally steering the plane to maintain height, direction and speed; it is done for him. This has not been provided so that the pilot can sit back, put his feet up and read his favourite book, *'When Zebras Discover Motorbikes'* – it has been done to enable him to apply his skills, knowledge and experience to more important matters. He might be monitoring all of the flight's systems, reviewing emergency procedures and getting more information about conditions on the route. This means he has the mental bandwidth to handle unforeseen issues and challenges such as technical malfunctions or the avoidance of storms.

Of course all of this relies on accurate and wise information being provided to the autopilot system because it will do whatever it is programmed to do. In extreme situations it will alert the pilot to an altitude or inappropriate speed issue but on the whole it only does what it is told to do.

In the same way your mindset will not run you, but in the absence of an override it will determine your 'way of working' by automating your approach and activities. It will be the 'unthinking routine' that you follow; it will be the 'default position' that you take; it will be the reactions and typical responses you have.

It is wise to frequently re-calibrate your autopilot.

In the light of this I am sure that you would agree that it makes good sense to thoroughly review what is programmed into your autopilot when you are at work. I would go as far as to say that it would be irresponsible not to audit the content, logic and principles that it is made up of. The best way of doing this is to create better awareness of what is actually programmed-in so that you can make some considered decisions about how you would prefer to act. This can be achieved by observing yourself, your choices and your reactions etc. so that you can notice what is happening by default. You can then of course make valuable decisions about some changes that you would like to see. To really accelerate this discovery process you could ask and answer the following question…

What is a helpful sales mindset?

I have suggested 5 key elements of a helpful and powerful sales mindset below and they are all about focus…

1. Focus on Focus
2. Focus on Professionalism
3. Focus on Persuasion
4. Focus on Opportunities
5. Focus on Technique

1. **Focus on Focus**

There are literally billions of stimuli demanding your attention at any one point in time. Obviously you have all of the internal communications going to your brain using your nervous system, through which information about your state of health and physical wellbeing is being continuously transmitted. You also have all of the external stimuli from your five senses sending information as you see things, hear them, feel them, smell them and possibly even taste them. Most importantly from our perspective you also have all of the cognitive processes going on. This is about all of your mental abilities and processes related to how you gather your knowledge and make sense of things. This also includes how you reason, how you identify problems and then all about how you solve them. This makes our brains pretty busy so a lot of that work goes on in the background; it is what is going on in the foreground that we need to consciously focus on.

Simply put, *focus is 'concentrated attention'*. It is about applying your attention with a conscious intensity; it can be described as a converging of awareness that brings better clarity, strength and impact. It is a wonderful faculty that can enrich your appreciation of things and enable you to have a significantly increased ability to influence things. When you are able to master the ability to effortlessly move between different types of focus you will find it an enabling and even liberating capability.

Focus is a word that is often used when looking at things through a lens. When you use binoculars to look at something, you focus them and bring the subject right close to you; it becomes the centre of your vision and consciousness. You can see the subject in a better light, in more detail and possibly even with better context. This is concentrated attention at work; it can take two forms being micro and macro.

Micro focus is all about zooming in and looking at things in fine detail. A microscope is a good example of this in action in that you can magnify things several hundred times and see what that the naked eye or typical view cannot see. In our context this could be about zeroing onto a specific person, business, opportunity, situation or event and engaging into the fine detail of it. Often it relates to things within the organisation.

By macro focus I am referring to an overall or bigger picture perspective. It is about how things relate in a wider sense and in business this will often refer to relationships and structures that the organisation has that are external to it. It could also refer to the wider market place and even the environment that the market operates in. Such a focus as this could be about valuing long-term customer relationships, valuing profit or the focusing on one set of products for strategic reasons.

Different job types focus their attention on different things, even in the same situation. What the Chief Engineer and the Chief Purser choose to focus on when they are at work on a luxury liner are very different. It is the same for you as a sales professional; what you choose to focus on will be different from others in your organisation and your sphere of influence. The important thing is to make it a considered and wise choice.

What is the 'locus of your focus'? Where is your focus mostly centred and why? Are you aware of it and is it a conscious choice? What is getting the benefit of your concentrated attention? If you can become acutely aware of this and make it a conscious and wise choice then you have the ability to significantly improve your performance. This is a vital element to creating an effective mindset because if you focus on being professional, having clear goals and looking for extra opportunities – you will do these things. Without this focus I have seen very capable sales people flounder and lose control over their meetings; they then become subject to the other person's agenda. Strive to make this an observable strength of yours. What gets your attention gets your action and energy; it allows you to helpfully channel your expertise. As you have limited reserves of these things it makes sense to value them highly and use them wisely.

Carefully consider the other elements of a strong and effective sales mindset which are outlined below and look for opportunities to focus on them.

2. Focus on professionalism

There are two ways of looking at the concept of being a professional and they both apply to you. We can talk about a musician being a professional musician meaning that this person earns their living in this way; we can also talk about them being a professional musician because of their superior skills and abilities. It is inferring that they are so good that they could indeed earn a living from doing it. It is a statement of credibility and high expertise. Most people reading this book will already be earning their living from selling (directly or indirectly) and it is the other concept of professionalism that I want to focus on i.e. as an approach and level of expertise. In this sense it is helpful to consider three different levels of expertise; Novice, Amateur and Professional.

It is quite easy to recognise the novice in the sales situation. They will be nervous and not sure that they are doing the right thing. This will easily transfer to the customer in the form of lack of confidence and uncertainty. Obviously this will hinder the sales process and the root cause of it is that the sales person does not, at this stage, know what they don't know. They don't have personal experience to draw on and unless they have made a concerted effort to develop their skills and techniques, they won't have any. It is important not to apply some sort of 'value judgement' to the position of novice because it is perfectly acceptable to be one. Nobody has been born with the skills and insight to immediately excel in the field of professional persuasion and we all have had to learn our craft starting as novices. Moving on from being a novice to an amateur is not just a function of time…it is a function of learning and development. This can take as long as you or others allow it to; it could also take as short as you are determined to allow it to.

The amateur sales person has learned much from being a novice and has developed some very helpful approaches and ways of working. They tend to have a few trusted techniques that they use well and often they get good results from them. In the same way that you can get some very proficient amateur musicians, you also get very proficient amateur sales people. They rely on their enthusiasm and optimism to get things done. They have transparent 'goodwill' which is attractive to buyers and their 'best of intentions' approach gets them cooperation and success. Their focus tends to be on making sure that they do not do things wrong as opposed to looking at how they can do things very much better. They will have basic skills and techniques but use them wisely. Their challenge is when they are faced with situations that their current learning has not equipped them for. The individual with the professional focus will see this not just as a challenge to overcome, they will see it as an opportunity to learn, develop and grow.

One of the things that hinders people from being more professional and obviously excelling in their role is that they are impressed with their current capability and they are not really looking to change it. They are not in the market for betterment and therefore they do not see or take advantage of the opportunities that are presented to them. The amateurs rely on their ability to *react* to circumstances and opportunities rather than an ability to *create* them. This is a shortfall that they actually see as a strength; it is like learning to manage problems well instead of learning to avoid them. They are comfortable in their comfort zone and consequently they stay there. The real risk for amateurs is that they think they have arrived at their appropriate expertise level rather than being on a continuous improvement journey to get there. One of the flaws of the highly experienced amateur is the propensity to always compare themselves to people who are not better than they are.

Complete the 6-point Professional checklist

There is a significant difference in the working practices of the professional as compared to the amateur and this is largely driven by a different mental approach. Consider the points below, how accurately do they reflect you?

- The professional is distinctly uncomfortable in any 'comfort zone'. They feel that if they are not stretching themselves then they are becoming stiff and inflexible.
- They value their agility and their flexibility and recognise that they have to have new experiences to develop further. They actively look for and create situations that will enable this.
- Professionals are self-driven with an urge to improve their skills, expand their knowledge and develop further capability. It is a sacrosanct imperative for them and it gives them the ability to convert day-to-day work into learning experiences.
- They take notes during meetings and afterwards they take time out to consider what went well, what did not go so well and what they would do differently if they had that interaction over again.
- The professional recognises that they need to develop a wide range of selling techniques that cover all of the stages of the selling process. They know that they need to be skilled in the

application of good techniques.

- They are not content with the concept of 'good' performance and see the need to convert good into exceptional.

For me the overriding evidence of professionalism is captured in the 5th point above. It points to the drive to develop an ever improving set of techniques and practices. This is more than attending training when requested; it is more than simply learning by experience. This is the purpose driven search for better ways of doing things. Great technique can provide a consistent and valuable competitive advantage and enable a consistency of achievement. It makes the best use of your energy and time as well as the opportunities that you face.

Even if you were acknowledged as the best 'putter' in the world in the game of golf…you could never become a professional unless you became proficient in the other elements of the game as well. There is no value being the best 'putter' in history if it takes you 42 shots to get to the green! In the world of sales this also applies. You may be a brilliant 'closer' but unless you can present products well or skilfully establish needs; you will not get the chance to use your expertise. It is great to have a unique talent at one of the techniques…but it is not enough if you want to excel in the profession. You need to have good expertise in a range of skills and techniques.

3. **Focus on Persuasion**

We talked earlier about 'Persuasion' being a key

element of the selling process and that without it you probably could not really call the interaction 'selling'. This is a key factor that separates the good from the great. The ability to construct a reasoned argument that provokes people to see things differently and inspires them to change their mind is an incredibly valuable talent. This is nothing to do with the 'gift of the gab'; it is more of a learned skill than it is a gift. When you are focussed on providing powerful points of persuasion rather than giving information you have the right focus. If you repeatedly do this you end up with a strong sales mindset. One of the first principles of persuasion is to consider the situation or opportunity from the other person's perspective so that you can understand what drives and moves them. This is not rocket science, it is basic psychology that takes place everyday in every home and business. If you focus on it however you can become proficient at it. It is perfectly acceptable to just 'take an order' when one is presented and all such opportunities are to be welcomed. Such easy sales situations cannot be relied upon however and they do not really constitute active selling.

Remember that with very complex sales you will only be selling a part of the overall business opportunity. You may have to persuade a certain group that the project represents real value for money. You may have to persuade a different group that your proposal mitigates the risks that they are concerned about. In another situation you may have to persuade key individuals that an investment in new machinery is a necessity and not a luxury. As you engage in this selling activity it all works towards the 'bigger picture sale'. In a more simple and straightforward situation you may simply have to persuade an individual to exchange his organisation's money for your product.

Successful sales people are driven by the need to persuade people and influence situations; they want to make an impact.

You can spot salespeople even when they are not at work. They are driven to make a difference by persuading people. They see disagreement as a challenge to overcome rather than a rejection to be avoided. This drive helps them to look for opportunities. Remember that data alone is not persuasive. You may throw a raft of information to a customer and unless it is analysed and meaning is extracted from it, then it will not be a persuasive argument. Even if your customer sees the argument that the figures are making, they still are helpfully influenced by a positive and enthusiastic presentation of the benefits that the data is implying.

4. **Focus on Opportunities**

A wise person once told me that there are only three types of people in business. You have a) the optimists, b) the pessimists and c) salespeople. According to his explanation you can always understand which is which by presenting them with the proverbial half glass of water. He noted that the optimist would see the glass as being half full and feel happy about it. The pessimist on the other hand would see the glass as being half empty and feel sad about it. The salesperson however would not be focussed on the water...they would be focussed on the part of the glass that does not have any water (yet). They would see an 'opportunity' to sell ice, more water or other things. They would see an opportunity and not just see a situation. A person with a sales mindset does not just make 'observations'; they tend to immediately convert an observation into a selling need. They use it as a platform from which opportunities can be recognised.

A situation or an interaction becomes an opportunity when you can see a way to add value or create demand. Whilst I certainly think that optimism is a helpful attitude; it is not an essential attribute of the successful salesperson. The pessimist might be able to identify objections more easily and then prepare compelling responses to them. Frankly it is the use of good techniques that separates the average performers from the good performers. Whether you consider yourself as an optimist or a pessimist means very little, it is just an unhelpful distraction and is not worth thinking about. Techniques for identifying commercial and strategic opportunities are worth spending time on and we will cover this in later chapters.

5. Focus on Technique

You are learning your craft and at some time you have engaged in the worthwhile journey from novice to amateur and from amateur to professional. Wherever you currently are in your journey, as well as the speed of your progress, it is all down to how well you are building up your range of techniques and developing your mastery of using them. I often meet with people who are highly motivated and they keep reading inspiring books and enjoy watching powerful clips of the worlds top speakers. They become even more fired up and enthused and this gives them energy and even more determination to succeed. On the whole this is obviously a helpful pursuit however I must raise a word of warning; if you are not careful this becomes counterproductive if it turns into a pursuit for the next emotional fix. Whilst it can develop in them an indomitable spirit of optimism and energy; this can only be temporary in itself. People are somewhat surprised when I say to them that it is time to stop doing this and to focus on developing their techniques, not just igniting their enthusiasm.

Please do not misunderstand what I am saying; it is good to access the motivational speakers and inspiring messages, in fact it is very good – it is just that it is not enough! That energy and enthusiasm, once it has reached fever pitch, needs to be channelled into wise techniques. It needs to be matched with proven ways of working. It needs to be supported by helpful approaches, processes and systems. The ambitious sales person needs to focus on developing their skills and the mastery of their craft.

You need to be a 'subject matter expert' in the art and science of selling and not just a 'subject matter expert' on your products.

These are not the same thing and they should both be diligently searched for. These are not matters for the mildly curious or those who set out to 'endure' their working lives. These are the things that convert good intentions into consistent good results.

The 5 key elements of a helpful sales mindset probably apply just as well to any career that someone engages in; they are however especially powerful in an environment in which you have to influence people. This is because a considered and purposeful outlook and approach will always yield better results than simply flying on an autopilot that was calibrated years ago. Having a strong focus will concentrate attention on the things that make a difference. A professional mindset will provoke the individual to do the right things right. Being persuasive and focussing on providing compelling reasons for others to agree with you is a vital ingredient to having influence.

Coaching Questions

Here are some useful 'thought-provokers' that relate to the application of a helpful sales mindset..

Consider the 5 key elements of a Sales Mindset. Which of these should you develop further? Which one is the priority for you?

1. Focus on Focus
2. Focus on Professionalism
3. Focus on Persuasion (selling)
4. Focus on Opportunities
5. Focus on Technique

How would you describe your personal Sales Mindset to someone else?

What words would you use? What might the overall message be? Think about how you responded to the above question; were you talking about an 'arrived destination' or were you talking about a journey?

How helpful to you is your current 'autopilot'?

What have you automated in terms of thinking and doing? What have you committed to autopilot that needs to be recalibrated?

How persuasive are you?

How would you know? Could you be more so? Spend some time asking people.

Are you skilled in developing 'points of persuasion'?

After a sales interaction can you readily tick off the different times that you were persuasive and what persuasive points you presented? Become known amongst your team and colleagues for asking the following question after a recent sales interaction... "What were the main points of persuasion that you used in that meeting?"

Suggested Activities

Consider the 6 point 'Professional Checklist' earlier on in this chapter. Make a note of the things that you do well and of the things that you should do more of. Set yourself some objective goals for you to work on over the next three months.

Intensely focus on the 'Points of Persuasion' principle and practice identifying them.
• Watch the news and listen to presentations; identify the points of persuasion that are used.

- Watch and listen to adverts – can you identify all of the points of persuasion that are being used, not just the obvious ones? Can you add further points?

Jonathan Frost

4

AN ENTERPRISING MINDSET
- YOU PLC -

This chapter provokes you to think about your own personal concept of 'work'. It is about how you frame it in your own mind; the way that you make sense of it. This actually makes a significant difference to your outlook in life and your approach to each day. It certainly is a strong factor contributing to the success that you enjoy (or don't enjoy!). I would suggest to you that right now is a good time to recalibrate your approach and select a different model to follow. This is a time to reset the autopilot.

Typically we see ourselves as employees i.e. someone employs us to do a job and in return for that activity you get paid a sum of money each month. You do your job and you get paid. This works for most people but does it really work best for you? Does this approach lead you to strive for improvement and a significant growth in capability? Does this approach accurately reflect your market worth or the contribution that you make? Does this approach encourage compliance or stimulate a driven excellence?

I would suggest that an employee mindset does not actually provoke you to be your best. One of the great benefits of being an employee is security. On the whole, your continued payment each month is secure, it can be relied on and this is a nice situation to be in. It will however influence your outlook and approach. I am certainly not saying that this is not a good influence but I am saying that it is not necessarily a good influence all of the time. A business often does not have such security and therefore it has to be agile and adaptive. It has to evolve and make changes if it is to grow, beat competition and flourish. A hybrid way of thinking could be seeing yourself as a 'contractor'. If you knew that you had to convince people to renew your contract every three months would this make a difference to your way of thinking? It certainly would! You would probably feel a continual need to impress and this would provoke you to ensure that you are 'obviously' providing value for money. The downside of this is that it might trigger you to think only about the short term; it could encourage you to avoid long term investment or courageous conversations because you have a renewal point coming up shortly.

Whilst 'employee thinking' is not a wrong approach in any way I would suggest that there is a more helpful and liberating way of thinking.

What if you were a business?

If you choose to see yourself well beyond the title of employee, manager or even leader and select a different 'model' to follow you will find it to be both rewarding and interesting. This is what I am referring to with the YOU plc analogy – I want you to think about yourself as if you were an actual standalone business. It is my experience that people have found this analogy and exercise to be a very powerful learning point however quite often they have not 'got it' first time around. The fact that it is so simple seems to detract from the huge value of this way of thinking; approach this methodically and slowly.

Firstly, if you were a business, you would need to have a *business model*. This is a line of thinking that you never go down if you are entrenched in an 'employee' mindset. It is probably the most important business concept that there is and simply put this 'business model' is the considered commercial process that is engaged in to generate profit; it is what the business actually does in exchange for money. The important element is at the end of the phrase 'for money'. It is not what the business does...it is what is does in exchange for money. You have to take a bit of an overview to capture this concept.

Let's apply this to an airline. What is the business model of an airline? It is to transfer people and goods from one location to another...and to charge much more than it costs. This can be a very complex process but essentially it boils down to that definition. Yes the airline does buy planes and hire pilots. It is true that they sell tickets and board planes. Obviously they takeoff and land planes – but why do they do all this? These things simply list what they do; the business model tells you why they do it i.e. they make money by charging a lot more than it costs them. They exchange the transportation of people and goods for money.

What is the business model of an internet search engine? It has to be more than just answering lots of questions and providing information. That would simply be a service model as opposed to a business model. In essence their business model is all about creating a website that millions and millions of people access everyday…so that it is a highly attractive opportunity to advertisers. They create a tremendous amount of 'click flow' and then exchange these created advertising opportunities for money. Of course they also capture valuable data and enable access to this in exchange for money.

What is the business model of a management consultancy? Yes it can be said that people come along and talk to people and have meetings. It is true that they bring in recommended systems and practices. They certainly encourage the business to adopt them and use them wisely. These are things that they 'do' however this is not the same as what their real business model is. Simply put, they exchange their skills, experience and expertise for money. This is how they make a living and whilst they may charge themselves out in units of time…it is not their time that they are selling. It is not their attendance at meetings that they sell – it is the results/changes/benefits of these meetings that they exchange for money.

What is your business model?

You need to have one! This question is directed at you personally and not the organisation that you work for. It has to go beyond what you actually do everyday; this is not about your Job Description. If you were a business - what would you be providing in exchange for money? It would not be your

'attendance' during working hours. You are not simply exchanging 8 hours a day for money (If you are by they way your approach is wrong and it will certainly be career and wealth limiting). Neither would it be about your availability for meetings, even if your attendance at them is mandatory. As valuable as it is to you personally, your organisation is seldom paying you for your product knowledge. Hopefully you have it and are using it…but that is not what your organisation is buying.
It would not be about the tasks and activities of your job description. It is not even the hitting of your sales target even though you are a sales professional.

You might think that the answer to the question is pretty obvious… 'my business model is to make sales and get paid a salary for doing it'. It just is not that simple. Your sales figures are as much dependent on others as they are on you. The Buying team need to select the right range and have purchased good quantities to satisfy demand. Marketing need to have promoted the right lines, through the right channels, to the right people. Logistics need to have efficiently stored the stock in a way that does not damage it, keeps it secure and ensures that it is readily accessible; they also need to deliver efficiently. We have not even mentioned yet some of the back office people who are needed in credit control, finance, fleet operations etc. So it would be way too simplistic to say that you are great because sales figures are high or that you are an incompetent because sales figures are low; we know the story is more complex than that.

So what is your personal business model? I would

suggest that it has 3 key parts to it…

1. Firstly it is to develop a relevant, valuable and rich portfolio of skills, knowledge and expertise *(this is your product range)*.

2. Secondly it is about wisely using this expertise to influence people, situations and results *(this is your service)*.

3. Thirdly it is to exchange this ability of yours to influence people for money *(the commercial transaction)*.

Your business model is to develop a powerful capability that others value highly and are prepared to pay for.

Your sales activities are the evidence of this capability. The things that you personally did to influence levels of business growth and customer loyalty are also evidence of your capability. The greater your proficiency in this area then the greater your value to your customer i.e. the organisation that you work for. Please don't just skim over this point; it is very important. Reviewing, developing and maximising your business model is your route to reaching your fullest potential.

Do you personally have a wide range of tools and processes that you use like a craftsman? Do you have proficiency in a wide range of techniques that your customer (i.e. your employer) values and needs? Are you continuously updating and expanding your expertise? As 'YOU plc' are you developing your product range and making it even more attractive to your customer base? Are you at 'expert level' in terms of your ability to influence situations and persuade people? Are you an acknowledged expert at understanding customer requirements and responding to them with compelling and persuasive solutions? Do you have a widely admired ability to present products in the most favourable way and stimulate buying decisions?

I do hope that the above questions were thought-provoking; do not worry if you could not answer an immediate 'yes' to each of them because this indicates opportunities for you to be even better. The final question would be... 'Are you maximising the commercial transaction i.e. are you being appropriately rewarded for your expertise?' As I mentioned earlier this is an extremely important concept that could be a real 'game changer for you – remember that your business model reflects the way that you have chosen to provide for your family and fulfil your dreams. This makes it very worthwhile to think carefully about and look for ways of adding value to YOU plc.

Businesses invest in people and products

A business is always looking to develop and stretch its portfolio of products so that it is continually relevant and attractive to its customers and potential customers. It wants to have what its customers are wanting; it also wants to convince its customer to want what the business has! Every business has to continuously evolve and adapt so that it can keep an advantage over its competitors. If it is not being agile and reinventing itself then others will simply 'out-innovate' it and take over from it.

If you think like an employee the above type of thinking is not relevant to you. Unless you are very ambitious, you don't focus on the competition to you personally (remember that we are not talking about the business that you work for). If you think like a plc however you will see the need to be innovative and to stretch your personal product range. It is well worth considering and answering the following questions...

'In what way have your skills been developed and enriched over the last 12 months?'

'In what way has your knowledge increased and become more valuable in the last 12 months?'

'In what areas have you established yourself as an expert at over the last year?'

You will notice that I have imposed a fairly short time frame in these questions. It could be argued that 12 months is not a long time however I would push back on this and say that improvement and strengthening needs to take place continuously and that progress should be evident even when looking back over a short timescale.

Businesses invest in research and development so that they can be at the cutting edge and so they can lead in their field. This same principle applies directly to you personally; you need to be aware of the latest selling techniques and engaged in learning about them. Here is an interesting question for you... "How much have you invested in yourself over the last year?" This is not about what courses your company has sent you on – it is about how much of your personal money have you invested in your expertise? If I were to ask the same question again...but make it over 10 years i.e. *'how much of your own money have you spent over the last 10 years developing your capability and expertise?'*...would the answer be any different? Does the level of this investment that you have made reflect the behaviour and approach of a person who is striving to excel and be recognised as a leading figure in your organisation and your industry? This is an important element of your business plan; it is a key differentiator between you and others.

Your business model i.e. your commercial business process requires you to have a complete range of skills, knowledge and expertise in order to make the model work. If you want to make it more than just 'work' and to actually excel and be widely recognised as superior...then you have to develop superior expertise. You need to have a respected, admired and flexible skills set. You need to have insightful and voluminous knowledge. For most people that represents a significant opportunity; for the successful people it represents 'work in progress'.

The second of the three key elements mentioned above about your business model talks about a practical application of this expertise and capability. Without this practicality your capability just becomes 'good potential' as opposed to 'good performance'. Remember that most customers don't want to buy just potential. You would not be happy to buy a big box of batteries and then to let them just sit on a shelf. You would want to use that potential; you would want to use those batteries to power up gadgets, lights and accessories.

As a sales professional your business model is

quite simple and involves the following;

It is about exchanging your abilities for money i.e. your ability to influence people to make decisions and take action.

It includes your ability to influence situations by converting them in to selling opportunities.

It also involves you delivering the results that are expected of you.

Your organisation greatly values your ability to persuade people to buy. It greatly values your ability to create situations in which their company and products are viewed favourably, leading to buying decisions. *It is this ability to influence that they are buying…not your time, skills or knowledge.* It is what you can actually do with these things that makes you valuable. They are buying your ability to make a difference when you interact with people and encounter situations. This ability is vital to you and if it is not your acknowledged strength, it needs to be. Is your customer getting value for money? Are there others out there doing it better than you?

Who is your main customer?

Any business needs to know for certain who their customer is as well as what they are looking to buy. If you think like a business then you need to consider these things as well. At first you may think that it is obvious; your customer is the person that you are calling on to win business. When looking through the prism of the 'YOU plc' analogy this is not quite correct. That person is actually your organisation's customer. External clients, end users or the public are actually your organisation's customers; they are not yours. The business that you work for is interacting with another business and you are simply the interface mechanism. Customers pay your organisation, they do not pay you. When they order...they are actually ordering from your company, not you. This is important because it provokes you to ask who then is your main customer?

I often hear sales people talk about them being the go-between between their employer and the customers of their employer. This is simply wrong. You only work for one side of that interaction; you only have one responsibility and that is to maximise the benefits that your employer/customer is looking to gain. You are not there to represent one side to the other and vice versa; you are there to persuade people to make decisions and take actions. The clue is in the title 'sales rep', it is about representing the company to the customer; this is not a two way representation. Such sales reps can be heard saying "I'm not sure my customers will like that" when introduced to a new system, process or practice. What they should be saying is, "I see the benefits of this to my organisation...how can I persuade customers of this?" If you represent a company's customers at the same time as representing the company then you are conflicted and will end up being of limited use to both sides.

Your real customer is the one who values your personal expertise enough to pay you money for it. Your customer is the one who greatly values what you can do and invests in ensuring that you have the right resources and opportunities to do it well; it is actually the organisation that you work for...not the one that you sell to. Your main customer is probably represented by your line manager and those in leadership. You need to discover what your customer and your main customer really values about you...and what they want you to achieve. It has to be more than just meeting a sales target.

How you sell, when you sell and to whom you sell are really important to your employer/customer. This involves aligning yourself to the company vision and mission; it includes abiding by and delivering the organisational values. It also involves contributing to the 'bigger organisational picture' and not just the short term sales gain perspective. It is not uncommon for successful sales people to be a little dismissive of rules and regulations and to 'push back' when they feel that they are being managed. This is not helpful and certainly not the perspective or position of the professional. It is much better to be focused on 'over-delivering' in the service that you provide to your employer/customer. It can also happen that sales reps get quite precious about what is and what is not their job; they don't always see the bigger business picture and if a task or event does not directly influence their sales figures then they show little interest. Again this is not an appropriate approach and certainly not one that is admired by sales managers and directors. They value contributions that make the overall business stronger and more successful and in the end this will increase sales opportunities too. It is quite difficult to see yourself through the prism of your real customer/employer however if you make the effort it can be hugely influential on your success, approach and outlook.

In essence your business plan involves delivering your part of your organisation's business plan. This requires much more than a series of regular 'sales interactions', it requires you to be a source of knowledge and insight, a provider of wise ideas and an impetus for action. Your personal 'business' (YOU plc) is to use your cleverly honed techniques to create commercial opportunities for your customer. *Your personal business is to enable and secure business for your customer.*

Businesses measure progress and success

Let us keep the analogy going to extract and further develop a more focussed and professional mindset. Most organisations are multifaceted and spread out. They have many people working away at tasks and these roles are interdependent. Strong processes, helpful collaboration and tight teamwork help the organisation to be efficient and productive. All of this does not happen simply as a result of luck; there is usually a habit of strong measurement of activities and results. This allows those in leadership to understand the realities of performance and react accordingly.

Typically an organisation will have four types of measurement and will measure progress through the use of metrics, effects, mindsets and behaviours; obviously these are all linked. Lets look at each of these and consider how you can apply them to YOU plc.

Metrics are the most common measurement and they could include sales figures, gross profit, margin, return on investment, stock-turn and a multitude of other figures. They tend to be preferred because they are tangible and make comparisons to different times or different organisations much easier. The metrics are often a common language that all in the organisation understand and use. It is important that you become fluent in this language of metrics so that you can easily understand the context that people are using to make decisions and this fluency also helps you to describe your world of services and benefits in terms that mean most to your customer/employer. Metrics can give you very helpful insight so that you can take wise actions and note 'early warning' systems. It would be helpful to thoroughly understand the current systems used in your organisation and especially how they are interpreted. You should note which are given prominence and why. It would also be especially helpful to develop an extra range of metrics that directly apply to your activities and results. Just because your organisation is not particularly interested in the wider measurement of an activity it does not mean that you should not be interested in it just for yourself. It might not be relevant to the whole organisation but it could be fundamental to you.

'Effects' are all about the impact of activities and behaviours. This is most popularly understood with the 'cause and effect' model and is all about understanding what triggers things to happen. If we see a ripple in a pond it is interesting to watch the ever increasing circles of water spreading out; it is more interesting to discover what actually caused it. For our purposes of having a sales mindset it is helpful to look at the effects that are taking place on our marketplace so that we can see what triggers them and then we can make some wise business decisions in response. Effects can point to the way that other people and departments are affected by an activity. A programme of change may have the effect of engaging people and enabling 'different' thinking. The cost-cutting programme may have the effect of driving efficiency and eliminating wastage. The remuneration and reward initiative may have the effect of increasing morale and securing the services of key people. You do however need to be aware of a popular concept when talking about cause-effect and that is the whole subject of 'unintended consequences'. Whenever an action is taken there will be both intended as well as unintended consequences and you need to be aware of this in your role as a sales professional. You need to have an acute awareness of what is actually happening out there is the sales field which might be quite different from what people intended to happen. A sales environment is very much the same as an eco-system in that there is a routine and reliability to the order and day-to-day practice. If you change this, just like an eco system, there could be many unforeseen and quite unexpected ramifications. The change programme mentioned above may actually create fear in some as well as the excitement I mention for others. Some may see it as a significant change to their preferred ways of working and may even start looking around for a new job. An unintended effect of the cost-cutting programme mentioned above could be that people stop spending money on really useful things and even stay doing things in an expensive and unproductive way. This is why it is very helpful to think about and clarify the 'effects' that you want to create and to look for meaning and 'root causes' in the effects that already exist.

As well as measurable metrics and observable effects there are also **mindsets** and **behaviours** that businesses try to foster in their organisation. These too are indicators of success that get measured and it might be about the entire workforce developing a collaborative approach that promotes and rewards strong teamwork and collegiate behaviour. It could also be a focus on profitability or a focus on outstanding customer service. Organisations need to influence and measure the mindsets and behaviours that determine their success.

Looking at things through a YOU plc filter provokes you to think about these things too. What metrics can you measure that will give you a helpful insight into your own progress and success? It is simply not good enough to 'let your sales figures do all the talking' because as we have discussed before they are never solely a result of your performance. There are a range of things that you could and should measure so that you have an objective and thorough picture. You might find it helpful to divide your own personal measurement into three key areas; Activities, Results and Approach.

Activity metrics could include...

- Number of sales interactions per week or day. How does this compare to others? What does this say about your work ethic? Are there too many to make them focussed...or are there too few to stretch you? I am sure that you can easily and convincingly explain your current practice however you should be looking to change things...not justify the current model.
- Conversion rates can tell you how many interactions are converted into a sale. What is your average? What is your best conversion rate for a month? What is your goal? What would a 'good' conversion rate look like for your industry? What would be an 'excellent' conversion rate? These are vital questions that businesses have to answer about their operations; it makes sense therefore that you do the same for You plc!
- Sales gestation periods can tell you how long it typically takes from initial interest through to delivery. Can you identify the things that delay or slow down the process? What would you like it to be and what influence can you exert to change it? What would a 'good' gestation period be?
- Average sales value. Quite simply you add up the total sales for the month and divide it by the number of business meetings that took place. Yes, it is a very crude measure and it does have many variables included in it; however if you are constant then it provides you personally with a metric that you can look to measure and improve. In many industries the sale is not definitely finalised during the sales interaction itself, people phone through orders or email purchase orders. Sometimes the order is made through an intranet.

This is why you add up the total sales for the period and calculate the number of business meetings that you have had. Customise this to make most sense to you. You might include phone calls as well.

Results metrics are common and often include...

-   Actual Sales figures. Often they are compared to target, budget and last year.
-   Trends. What is the trend? Are things getting better or not over time? What is the trend for product/service categories; what do individual product trends tell you? What actions are you being self-prompted to take in response?
-   Percentage contributions of the different product or service segments that you sell. Do you know where your business is coming from and have you considered how to ignite sales of slow performers?
-   Margins. Is it your stated goal to maximise margins or maintain them? What is the trend and how do you personally act in response? It is not really appropriate to say that you are waiting for instruction or clarification about what your customer/employer wants...your role is to discover it and deliver it.

Approach indicators could include...

-   How are you received by your customers? Are you welcomed? Do people see good commercial reasons to meet up with you? Do you find your sales interactions to be collaborative or competitive? Is somebody trying to win when you are meeting; is it gladiatorial? It should be a case that you are working together to create and deliver a commercial opportunity that suits you both.

- Do the people that you engage with respect you? It is important to earn respect but it is also appropriate to expect it and raise the matter if it is not given. I sometimes see that a sales person's time is not respected and they are unreasonably kept waiting or meetings are cancelled at the last minute. Often this represents a respect issue and you have to dig into this to discover the root cause and fix it.

- Do you have influence? It is common for people to be fixated on that true but old fashioned and inadequate truth that people will buy from you if they like you! Yes it will be easier but it is nowhere near enough to be relied on never mind being a conscious tactic. It is a given that you are a nice person, you are easy to talk to and that you have good social skills. It is a starting point not an end point. Influence means that you can sway their thinking and convince them to take actions. Influence means that they value your knowledge, approach and your commercial expertise. It means that you have a persuasive effect on them and their thinking.

- Sphere of Internal Influence. This is a very important concept to a business like you. How big is your sphere of influence? How many people in the organisation that you work for do you have a strong and influential relationship with? Can you draw on committed and friendly assistance from individuals in marketing, sales support, logistics and finance? Do you have a circle of people who actually empower and enable you because of their position and resources? You need to convert this from a concept into a plan. Make lists of your current sphere and identify people who you would like to establish a mutually helpful relationship with. This is not a matter of using people or manipulating them; you all work for the same organisation and you are all engaged in making it successful.

- Sphere of Customer Influence. The 'customers' that you sell to most probably belong to the organisation that you work for. A YOU plc mindset however also sees these customers as people assets of *your* business. You need to have a database of people so that you can form strong and influential relationships. How many of these relationships do you currently have? Is it enough? Does that number reflect a driven and dynamic business owner? How big should it be? Remember that we are not talking about organisations, we are talking about individuals who work in organisations. Your asset is the relationships that you have with people because they bring about influence.

I am both amazed and horrified when individuals tell me that they do not engage in any of the above because their company does not provide the data. These same people often tell me that they don't like administration or providing reports from which all this data could be gathered. I am suggesting that as a business owner you look to do what would be helpful for YOU plc and engage in activities that give you feedback about your performance and progress; this will help you to become more valuable and marketable as an individual. Have a powerful sales mindset and be so much more than just an employee.

So we see that there is much value in looking beyond the typical perspective of being an employee. If you see yourself as a business and conduct yourself accordingly you will find that you accelerate your personal development and success. As you adopt your business model as the main driver for your career you will notice and even create opportunities to significantly enhance your position and your earnings. All good businesses constantly review their product portfolio and look for ways to innovate and add to it. Your product portfolio is made up of your skills, knowledge and experience; you want to keep enriching these products. You want to innovate and add-value to your commercial proposition by adding to your expertise. What does the 'Annual Report' look like for YOU plc? Are you measuring your success and your progress? As you hold yourself accountable to financial and non-financial metrics (as outlined earlier) you will have the energy and momentum to see you through the inevitable difficult times. Some businesses are enjoying rapid growth, some are experiencing a period of significant change and others are restructuring and re-engineering in a fight for survival. It will be the same for YOU plc, you will experience a mix of situations along your journey and the secret is to de-personalise the situation and take the emotion out of it. As a business you carefully and objectively analyse the situation and develop a strategy to remedy it.

Thought provokers

Here are some useful 'thought-provokers'. They relate to the application of an entrepreneurial mindset

In what way have you developed your skills, knowledge and experience over the last 12 months?
What have been your biggest gains?

What is your business model?
What service do you exchange for money?

How much time do you spend investing in your expertise (product range)?
This would include reading books, talking to mentors, watching video clips etc. There are a whole host of free and paid resources on the internet – they include audio books, podcasts and interest groups on social media.

How many people have asked you to mentor them?
The answer to this question gives you good insight into how your professionalism and expertise is acknowledged by those around you.

Do you have a 'business plan' that increases the value of You plc?
This might be about communication, negotiating, open questions closing etc.

What do your metrics say about your personal performance and progress?

Should you be doing more to measure your activities, results and approach?

Suggested Activities

It makes good sense to align yourself to people who have the same vision and determination to develop their expertise and to significantly increase their market value.

Set up arrangements to coach each other during phone calls. Create a network of associates who will ask helpful questions (fine examples are provided in a later chapter) so that you encourage each other and inspire each other to excel.

Start a podcast club or book club with a group of associates. Discuss a business book or listen to a short podcast together and then extract learning points. It is fun to do this with a small group of you and being accountable to the others will help with consistency of action. This can be a useful networking business lunch as well.

In your reading and development activities be sure to focus on techniques and not just the motivational type of experience.
- Create a list of techniques that would be useful
- Prioritise the list according to those that will give you the best return on your investment of time
- Schedule a technique a week for two months and then set out to practice them
- Do not judge yourself on any failure...rather use up your energy celebrating your progress so far

You can convert your day-to-day experiences into learning experiences if you use the '3 Review Questions' after every sales interaction...

1. What worked well in that interaction?
2. What did not work so well?
3. What would I do differently next time?

Be sure to set up a 'metrics checklist' so that you can measure your performance and progress. Be creative, whilst some examples are provided in this chapter your own situation may make different metrics more appropriate. Be sure to keep records, set up a spreadsheet for comparisons and understanding trends. Remember this is about *your* performance not the performance of the organisation that you work for.

5

A 'VALUE-ADD' MINDSET

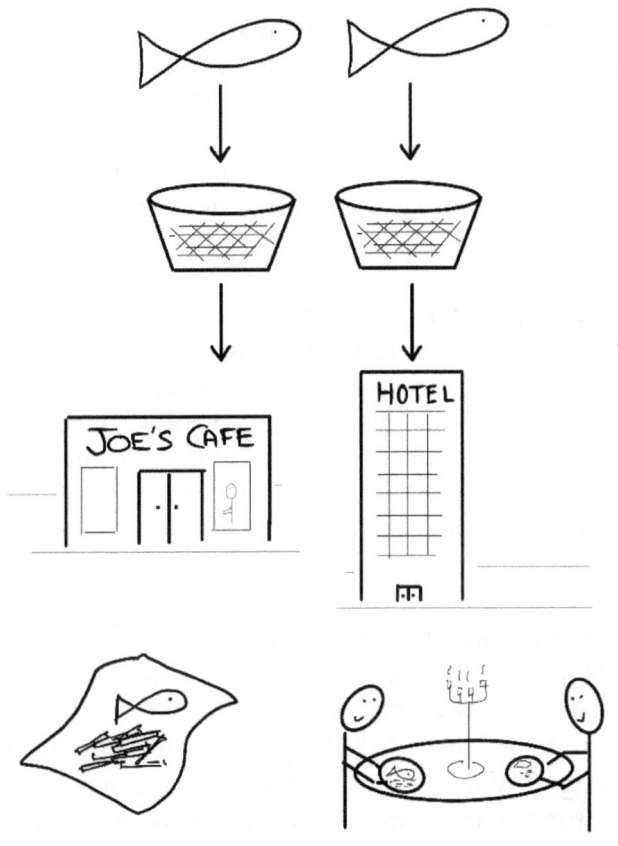

How much is a dead fish worth?

A correct but woefully inadequate response to this question is often 'it depends'. This is actually a very important business question and whilst it might not be asked in many sales training programmes it is well worth thinking about. The concept of 'product value' is extremely important to your working world and if the perceived value 'depends'…make sure that it depends on you as much as possible!

The image on the previous page outlines the 'two fish story' – can you work out the important business message?

It is a simple analogy to explain the concept of added value; this is a powerful element of a sales mindset. Over the years many of my clients have found this to be an especially illuminating and helpful concept and I hope that you do as well. Essentially to be better than others at what you do, you have to do different things or do things differently; this adds value to your offering.

I have included the typical line drawing that I use to explain it and I am fully aware of how technically poor it is as a drawing. It is not meant to be anything other than a visual to help to communicate the message. When you start drawing it and building up the story your audience becomes fully engaged and this helps them to remember the message and be able to explain it to others. We know that in selling it is wise to use visual aids to guide the customer through a journey of discovery. People tend to discover how appropriate and relevant your message is if they can 'see' it as well as 'hear' it. Drawings like this act as that visual aid and funnily enough the more professional the drawing the less helpful the image becomes. In the early days I had a cartoonist draw some of my analogies for me and they were certainly a superior piece of art however the difficulty was that in the pre-packaged visual people 'looked' at a journey rather that 'took' a journey; when I tested the different approaches the poor but 'live' drawings were always preferred to the professional work. Please feel free to draw it yourself as you explain this important concept to others.

Consider the following short story…

Two fish are swimming in the sea. They are identical twins; this means that they have exactly the same genetic structure, they are the same in everyway.

One day they are both caught up in the nets of a trawler.

The trawler lands its catch at the docks and for the first time in their lives the two fish are separated. One goes into basket (A) on the left hand side and the other goes into basket (B) which is on the right hand side.

Basket (A) is sold to a fish merchant who sells his fish in London. He sells this particular twin fish to 'Joe's Greasy Café' in the East End. It is taken into the kitchen and in due course is battered, fried, given some chips and wrapped in cheap grease paper. It is served to the next person in the queue as a 'fish supper' - for the princely sum of £2.99

Basket (B) is sold to a fish merchant who also sells his fish in London. He sells this particular twin fish to the well-respected and envied 'Balmoral Hotel'. It is taken to the kitchens and in due course is lightly grilled, presented on a plate with new potatoes and green peas and is served in the restaurant. The restaurant is well known with attentive staff, soft music and plush surroundings. This 'fish supper' is delivered to the table – and costs the diner £29.90

The '2 Fish Analogy' is designed to provoke thought about 'value'. How much is a dead fish worth? We have acknowledged that 'it depends' and this section is all about what it 'depends' on and how this should influence your sales approach. Remember that these fish are identical twins i.e. they are the same in every single way. Despite this, one sells for ten times the amount of the other. What has happened here?

When discussing this with a group of sales people they often respond very quickly with an explanation about the higher overheads at the hotel. It is suggested that because they have higher costs they have to charge higher amounts. This is true but it does not account for a tenfold difference. I usually ask how many people in the room are prepared to pay extra because just the business they are buying from has extra costs – not many people say yes!

The discussion usually moves on to explain the

difference in terms of the offer; you are paying for the nice building, in a great location with superb ambience. Nice people, attentive staff and background music all cost money and this has to be passed on. Again this is true in part – but it does not explain the real difference i.e. why would you be prepared to pay extra for these things?

A very significant process has taken place in these two businesses - 'Added Value'. This is at the very heart of our economic world because so much of our economic behaviour is driven by what we value. If someone or something adds value i.e. makes it more valuable to us, it can readily influence a change in our approach and behaviour. The two fish are identical however the hotel 'added value' to the product. At Joe's Greasy Café a dead fish is worth £2.99. At the Balmoral Hotel a dead fish is worth £29.90

We start off with two identical fish swimming in the sea. The fact that they are identical in every way is important because the difference in value at the end of the day is not due to there being two different products; it is actually due to the 'adding of value' to the very same product. In the same way that there are many fish in the sea there are also many products in the market place. There are products, services, ideas and concepts that are identical to the ones that you are selling and you need to have a differentiator to stand out for the crowd; you need to add value to it to make it special. Remember that you are not just competing with your own competitor's products, you are also competing with the many different ways that customers can choose to spend their money.

Most of us are not selling products or services that people absolutely need in order to survive. Most of us are actually selling 'wants' – we are offering things that people want; the risk is that they may suddenly discover something else that they want instead!

People who buy from you have a choice. They can choose not to buy, choose to buy something else completely or choose to buy a competitor's product. Your role as a persuader is to create a circumstance in which people will choose to buy your products from you. If you truly cannot add any value to *what* you are selling then you need to add value through *the way* that you are selling it. If you are thinking like a business as opposed to thinking like an employee you will be spending/investing time evaluating about your own business processes. This will include looking at what you are providing as well as the way that you are doing it.

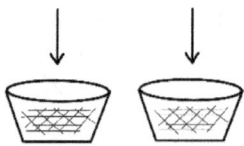

"...they are both caught up in the nets of a trawler".

The fish have been captured; this part of the story relates to a point in time or a situation where your persuasion has resonated. It has had a response; to continue the fishing analogy there is a bite on the bait. This might mean that there is a sympathetic and curious ear to your concept or proposal or it could be that your customer sees and understands your solution to their problems and they want to know more. Obviously this could be an incoming enquiry or a request for quotation. In essence an 'awareness' of your offering and the benefits of it has taken place.

This is an important stage of the selling process and you are probably not in direct control of it. In the trawler analogy the fish can become damaged in the nets and when this happens you lose the value of it because nobody wants to buy damaged goods. In the same way an enquiry can be handled poorly and the customer is discouraged rather than encouraged to do business with your organisation. In this case the very first POCI (point of customer interaction) is compromised and that makes the rest of the process tougher. It can also happen during meetings when the customer talks about their business and this provides selling opportunities...but the sales person is not listening attentively and buying signals are not captured or noticed. This is the equivalent to the trawler spilling its nets back into the sea when trying to load them on board.

It is wise to carefully look at the processes involved in capturing leads and sales opportunities; you need to ascertain if things slip through the net and whether the company makes full use of those initial points of customer interaction. How highly are leads valued in your organisation? You can evaluate this by the emphasis they get, the resources allocated to secure them and the infrastructure in place to trigger them. We talked earlier about the need for you to know and influence the sales process and auditing how leads are captured and distributed is always a good place to start. If it is not as effective and productive as it needs to be in your organisation then an internal selling process needs to take place. You need to persuade key people to make decisions and take actions to make this a strength. Selling ideas and concepts internally is a key element to building a sales environment so that you can benefit from a healthy corporate sales mindset.

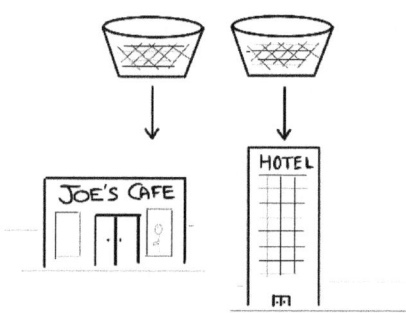

Basket (A) is sold to a fish merchant who sells his fish to 'Joe's Greasy Café' in the East End.

It is important not to get judgemental or snobbish about different business models. It is very easy for businesses to get all excited about premium products but we should remember that one business model is not superior to another because of the price of the goods, they are just different. They are designed to attract different markets and customer segments. Joe's Café knows what their customers want and they provide it admirably. Whenever we have a focus on added value it is essential that we do not see this in terms of money alone, we must see it through a customer's perspective. Joe's customers have four main drivers; food that is hot, food that has taste, food that makes you feel full and food that is inexpensive. This is what is important to them. The addition of soft lighting and ambient music is not going to add any value to them. They will not appreciate waiting and will be unmoved by the formal dress of waiters. They don't value being waited on but do value being served quickly. Joe's Greasy Café has certainly added value to a dead fish. It has converted it into a valued fast food product that sells in volume and is profitable. We call this business success.

It is always wise to look closely at the business model of your customers and understand the drivers of their customers. What are their internal drivers? What provokes them to see things the way that they do and act the way they do? What do their customers value? How are they trying to add value? This thinking will help you to be relevant and align yourself much closer to their working world; it could position you to have favour and see opportunities that others may miss.

Basket (B) is sold to a fish merchant who also sells his twin fish to the well-respected and envied 'Balmoral Hotel'.

The Balmoral Hotel has targeted a different market and their customer base is quite different. It could be said that they have a more difficult task because the needs of their customers are more complex. They have both internal and external drivers. Their internal drivers are all about enjoying hot and tasty food. They want a dining experience that is different to day-to-day meals and one that engages their delight in strong flavours. They look for experts to blend ingredients to create something special.

They also have external drivers which are all a part of the desired experience. This includes being treated in a certain way. Whilst Joe's customers are relatively ambivalent to the way they are treated as long as it is not discourteous or rude, The Balmoral's customers have strong expectations. They often want to feel valued, important and special. The décor, staff uniforms and manner in which they are treated are an integral part of the experience. These diners want to be seen to be doing well and to mix with nice, refined people who are also doing well. They know that to make this happen they need a fairly exclusive environment and high prices create this. So we see that The Balmoral has added value to a dead fish by converting it into a gourmet dinner. It has added further value by making it a superior experience, something that some people value highly and will pay more for. They then added even more value by creating an exclusive environment which people want to be seen in.

What added the value?

We know that the two original base products, 'dead fish', were identical; one however ended up having a value of ten times the other. I would like to prime you to think about this quite carefully. The whole focus is not really about the Balmoral Hotel, the focus of all this is about you! How well are you adding value to what your customer's experience? Are your products and services perceived to be more valuable because of the way that you do business?

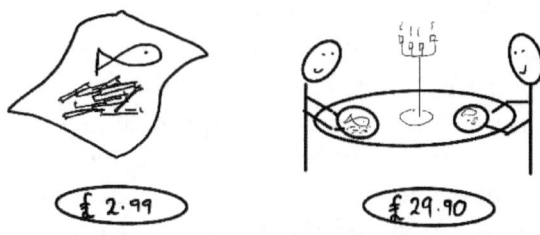

It is important to ask what added the value because it is a very powerful activity in our working worlds. We probably agree that adding cost does not necessarily add the value, so what does? *It is the customer's experience that added the value from their perspective.* The two different customers certainly had very different expectations of their visit and these would be based on the 'expected experience' that they were going to have. In actual fact it is not so much about specifically what the customer's experience…it is about how they *perceive* that experience – how they make sense of it and value it. As they experience their interaction with the company and the products that they receive, they start forming judgements and these all add up to a general 'feeling' about things. If it is positive then value has been added. The additional costs of décor, staff, and environment are incidental if the customer does not perceive them to be positive and valuable. It is not so much their experience but the perception of their experience that actually adds the value.

So when was the value added? I think it is fair to say that value was being added early on as soon as the fish were caught and then sold to the merchants.

Right at the start the one fish merchant had different ideas for his 'end product'; he had determined a smarter way to sell his fish, to someone who would be prepared to pay more. Whilst value was added along the way…it was not equally added at different stages. It is interesting to note that the stage that had most influence was at the point of customer contact. It is at the 'point of interaction' that the much value is added. The Hotel took the same raw product (a dead fish) as the Café; but took it through a different process and presented it differently. This culminated in a more valuable experience to the customer.

What assumptions have been made about added value? There is of course a very large assumption that we have made so far. We have assumed that a dead fish is worth £2.99 at the beginning and that the Hotel added to it. What if a dead fish is actually worth £29.90 and the Café took value away?

The very same process that we discussed before can work in reverse. What the fish went through (batter, wrapped in newspaper, customers having to queue etc.) was not as valued by the customer. Their experience reduced the value they placed on the product and this was represented in the price that they were prepared to pay. If £29.90 was the accepted value of a dead fish – it was not to those customers of Joe's i.e. value had been taken away by the experience of the customer.

So we see that people are influenced by their experiences. We see from this analogy that what people experience…either adds value or takes value away. Whilst this has obvious learning points for businesses and the development of business models it also has a significant point for sales professionals as they engage in influencing people, situations and results. Your interactions with others have the potential to 'add value' to you as a person to do business with. They can build your personal brand and deepen commercial relationships. Your interaction style and presentation can give you direct relevance and ensure that your proposition is given due attention and gravitas. If their experience of you is one that is relevant, motivating and enlightening then you will always be welcomed and always listened to; you have added value to YOU plc. By doing this your significance to your customer will be greater and more obvious. You will have a stronger influence and be in a position to make a more meaningful contribution. Unfortunately the opposite is also true. The relevance and significance of your message can also be diminished by people's experiences of their interaction with you. Think carefully about this when you are preparing and executing your meeting strategy. Think about this in terms of all of your emails and correspondence with customers. What are you saying? The messages that you are unconsciously giving are just as relevant and impactful as the messages that you actually mean to give. Your reputation (brand value) is a direct result of the consistent experience of you that others have. It is not at all about avoiding doing things wrong, it is all about doing that which is valued in the eyes of the customer.

You probably do not sell dead fish for a living

however you probably also don't have a monopoly or a totally unique product. Customers have choices and what you provide almost certainly has twins out there. These 'twins' are other products, services and experiences that are available and in essence are the same as yours. How can you add value? What can your customers experience that makes them feel your contribution is more valuable than others? It might be in your working processes or your presentation. It could be all about your superior 'subject matter expertise' and it could even rest in the helpful and commercial environment that you create. However you set out to do it you definitely need to be obvious and consistent. Without any form of added-value you will definitely lose competitive advantage and this will make your role much more difficult. Remember that the difference may well have to be in the way that you do business rather than the products or services that you provide.

Thought provokers

Here are some useful 'thought-provokers'. They relate to the application of a value-add mindset

How well do you really understand the experience of customers and what they value?

How do you gather this information? It is very easy to just see things through your own particular prism of experience and to understand approaches and activities from your own organisation's perspective. Remember that what you do and how they perceive it is always adding or subtracting value;

make this a conscious influence on your choices.

What do your organisation's customers really value in terms of the following and how could you further add-value to them?
Personal experience
Business process
Products and services

What do your competitors and challengers do differently to you?
What messages do you take from your answer?

Suggested Activities

It is well worth spending some time considering the mechanisms you use to communicate and engage with customers. Make a full and detailed list of all the different types of interactions. When you have done this consider each of them individually in terms of the three questions below...

- What 'value' do people place on these events and activities?

- What does the £29.90 version look like i.e. what does a great experience look like?

- What would a £2.99 version look like? How far away from this are you?

Jonathan Frost

6

AN ENGAGED MINDSET

Previously when we looked at professionalism we did so from three different perspectives; the novice, the amateur and the professional. We noted that the outlooks and approaches of people at these very different levels would have significant differences and that we should be aware of this in our interactions with them. It is also helpful to talk about engagement in terms of three different levels and this chapter will explain them and provide a useful model to sense-check your mindset. As a subject this is highly important to the sales professional because an enhanced level of engagement is a clear way to differentiate yourself and it makes your job much easier. Your job is definitely much harder if you are not engaged and this is because it takes effort to 'think on the hoof' and 'ad-lib' your way through meetings. It takes more mental energy to be constantly alert for risks and problems just because a clear plan with a good set of tactics had not been considered. Think about yourself setting out on a long journey in your car and only 30 minutes into it a warning light flashes up on your dashboard, it is telling you to check your tyre pressure. You have a another 35 miles to go to the nearest service station and so you continue your journey. You are hyper sensitive to every judder of the steering wheel, you are acutely conscious of all sounds and you keep scanning the signals and behaviours of other road users. You are using this state of hyper-alertness because you cannot feel in control; something could happen at any minute. By the time you reach the service station you are exhausted and it is the longest half hour of your year. This is what it is like to not be engaged enough to prepare enough.

Engagement is all about involvement and participation. It hints at an active connection and interaction with something. If I am 'engaged' in a discussion you would see me as an active participant however if I was not engaged in the discussion you would see me as remote and more like a spectator. In the context that we are talking about this is also all about the intensity of commitment, energy and bandwidth. To be engaged in something means to personally make a difference.

When a couple become engaged it is a public statement of commitment and long-term intention. It follows an active deepening of the relationship and is the result of a strong and mutual attachment. Being engaged in this instance makes all the difference to the relationship and the future.

When you are in a car and you engage first gear it gives you the opportunity to use all the power and technology within it to drive forward and make progress on your journey. The vehicle has the potential to go 100mph but until the gear is engaged it is going nowhere!

In your working world of persuasion and influence you need to be thoroughly engaged in your mission. You need to be committed to it and consistently apply all of your resources and energy to make progress. It is often a clear differentiator between sales people; it is something that is always on the radar of professional buyers and others that you meet. It is commonly called 'passion' however I prefer to use the term 'engaged' because it is more businesslike, less emotional and it has a wider application.

A useful analogy to sense-check your levels of engagement is to consider the scene of a typical day on the beach. The sun is shining, the sea is beautiful and the sand is white and soft. The main attraction is the turquoise warm water and the stated goal of everyone attending is to swim in the lovely sea *(humour me here, I know that there are many other reasons why people go to the beach...but not in this story!)*. As you sit back on your deck chair you look around and notice that there are four types of participants in the beach experience.

Some are lying on the sand soaking up the sun, reading a book or chatting with their friends. They are enjoying themselves and are participating in the event but they are not engaged in the mission to swim in the sea. They are happily disengaged in 'the' mission; but they are very engaged in a parallel mission i.e. to enjoy the day.

Others are paddling in the water. They are ankle to knee deep and are experiencing the water flow around them and feeling the sand shift beneath their feet. It is a good feeling and they look quite pleased with their experience so far. They are engaged in the mission although it cannot be said that they have enthusiastically embraced it at this point in time.

You also note that there are waders; people who have extended beyond paddling and the water is around their waist and even up to their chest. This seems to be a bit of a temporary situation because there are not that many of them. People tend to paddle or go right in; you don't see that many people wading around and when you do they do not seem all that happy with the experience. They have gone beyond the pleasantness of the sea around their ankles and the feeling of sand running beneath their feet...it has become unsteady and not so much fun. The water does not seem as warm around your mid section and chest and the currents and waves are hard to overcome. You have to work hard to fight your own buoyancy and very quickly you decide to dive in and start swimming.

This is the final group you see from the comfort of your deckchair. The swimmers are splashing around and having lots of fun. Some swim strongly to exercise and achieve distance, others try to out-swim the waves and a few try to float gently and relax in the water.

As you would expect I would like to draw on this analogy to provoke further thought about the whole topic of engagement. I do see the 'paddlers' out in the sales field; they will do what is asked of them and do their best to be busy during office hours. They are definitely a part of the sales experience, they are in the water, but they are not engaged in the mission. Such people often find themselves going through the motions, making the sales calls and capturing the available orders. They have their routine and see consistency and loyalty as their greatest strength. Often their mantra is "my customers trust and respect me" and they act to make sure that there is no reason why customers should not buy. I would see these people as being aware of the mission but not really engaged in it with any sense of commitment or enthusiasm. They will turn around and see others who are still lying on the beach and rightly recognise that they themselves are much more engaged than those asleep in the sun. The paddler has a consistent view of sales performance; when sales are down it is because of the difficult economic climate and when sales are good it is because of their outstanding sales ability. The paddler often has much time to dwell on what is wrong in their working world and makes sure that everyone hears their concerns and observations.

The waders are not looking back at the paddlers; they tend to look forward to the swimmers. This is the direction that they are going as they further immerse themselves in the task at hand. These are the sales professionals who are working hard to improve and are discovering better ways of doing things. They make themselves vulnerable by trying out new approaches and techniques and are impatient for success. Before meetings they will think hard about approaches that they could take and situations they may face. They will prepare facts and figures to back-up their arguments and will look for compelling sales points that they can present. Whilst they are not as fluid and smooth as the swimmers they are fully engaged and committed; their challenge is to match their enthusiasm with techniques and proven processes.

The swimmers are the fully engaged. Their feet have left the ground and they are probably too deep now to put them down anyway. They have lots of movement in the water and can be agile to change direction and take a new approach whenever they like. If necessary they can swim fast and far or they can ride the waves and play. They are confident in their swimming technique to be alert to new opportunities for fun and they can set the pace. These are the sales professionals who are thoroughly engaged in the mission and have committed themselves to making it fun and making it work. Such people will establish compelling goals before a meeting and will remain alert during conversations to buying opportunities. They tend to manage a territory rather than simply call on their current customers. They will adopt the 'YOU plc' way of thinking and be entrepreneurial in their approach. They will never be clock watchers but they will value their time.

So we see that when talking about engagement we can refer to paddling, wading and swimming. This is all about immersion in the mission. Are you in it up to your ears? During your working day are you 'in the zone'? This is about giving your available consciousness to the job that you are doing and having the courage to look for ways of doing it better. This is not at all like 'obsession' which is a very unhelpful attribute. The engaged person has a helpful focus that includes peripheral vision and contextual understanding. The obsessed person has a specific fixation and this blocks out context and wisdom. You do not want to be obsessed with your job, a specific technique or a particular goal; you do want to be fully engaged in your mission.

The Formula for Engagement

There is another useful mechanism that you can use to provoke helpful thought about the whole issue of engagement and if you have read a previous book of mine called 'When Zebras Discover Motorbikes' you will recognise the formula; I have applied it slightly differently here.

Engagement level = (E+A+R)a

The **'E'** refers to the amount of effort that is applied to your role and your mission. This is the perspiration rather than the inspiration and it is patently obvious that someone could not be described as fully engaged if they are not expending loads of energy. For the sake of this formula we are not putting a 'value judgement' on the effort...we are putting a judgement about the intensity or amount of it. A very hard working individual who is not getting good results is much easier to help and change than a lazy individual who is not getting results. It should be an absolute 'given' that people work hard and apply lots of energy. Selling is a profession that uses a lot of energy because it is hard work to interact with people and engage them to see things differently and think differently. You have to develop and use both mental stamina as well as physical stamina. Having said that I am certainly not an advocate of working extremely long days and spending lots of time working over the weekend. It is my experience that high performing sales professionals are actually quite human so when they do too much they get tired and this impacts on their enjoyment of the job as well as their results. Tired people cannot be alert people and they will find it difficult to be innovative and clever. I am talking about being fully engaged and 'in the moment' when working and then totally turning off when you are not. Expanding your day to get everything done is a slippery slope that can negatively impact your sales figures. It masks a problem that should really be addressed. The problem might be that there is simply too much to do and the department needs to restructure its work allocation to enable everyone to do what they have expertise in doing. We don't want doctors driving the ambulances and we certainly don't want ambulance drivers doing the surgery; so this may point to a need to reallocate work. Long working days and weekend working might however point to issues of efficiency and productivity. Are you chasing to be as efficient as you can be? Do you engage in passive resistance when it comes to administration routines and computer processes or do you look for ways to save time when doing them? Using your scarce resource of energy wisely may mean that you have to be better at prioritising and planning. You might have to be a lot more self-critical about the choices that you make about how you spend your time. You may have to be more assertive with yourself and others so that you do the things that you should be doing and not just the things that you like doing. These are tough introspection points however you have to do it to be truly professional. The problem with extending your day and your week is that you will eventually run out of both. Don't start this journey because you won't like the final destination. It is wiser to place great value on your energy and time and be ruthless in how you use it. Value your personal time too and don't confuse the two.

Engagement level = $(E+A+R)a$

The **'A'** stands for the activities that you undertake. This is about how well and wisely you use the effort mentioned above. Sheer effort and energy alone will not give you the results that you want because you need to engage in the specific activities that influence people and situations; it is these wise activities that create results. It is all about doing the right things and doing things right; whilst good intentions and approaches are very helpful (and good attributes to have) they cannot alone get you the success that you want. There has to be a very direct correlation between the actions that you take and the results that you see. This 'cause and effect' principle can work very well for you if you have the right action/cause to take. This is why you need to consistently audit your skills, tactics and capabilities. In the next chapter you will find a very helpful self-assessment tool; how well you engage in it is directly proportional to how 'engaged' you are in the furtherance of your career and your future. Self-assessment, whilst not always comfortable, is a very helpful activity to engage in. It is important not to value 'being busy' unless it is being busy doing the activities that bring you success. We also talked earlier about the need for you to learn new skills and techniques because these are the activities that you should be engaged in. Doing 'something' is not good enough for the high performer.

In and earlier chapter we agreed that your organisation is not paying for your effort…they are paying for results or the 'effect' that you can have.

The sort of activities that you should be engaged in definitely include creating an energetic and dynamic sales environment. You should be thoroughly engaged in creating sales opportunities as opposed to merely reacting to them. You should be engaged in the activity of creating powerful business relationships, engaging in influential meetings and presenting products in a way that compels customers to buy.

An indicator of your engagement is the level of 'purpose' that you have in all that you do; especially for business meetings. An engaged sales person is passionate about taking action to persuade people to make decisions and take actions. Another indicator of engagement is the activity that goes into developing your skills, knowledge and techniques.

Engagement level = (E+A+R)a

The **'R'** stands for the Results that you enjoy/suffer. The massive effort and activities that you employ must work together to make a difference to the results. If they do not then there is little point in your engagement. It is recognised that there are many areas that affect the results over which you do not have any direct control and that is why you really need to major on the things that you can directly influence.

One of the things that you definitely can influence is your attitude and approach. This is what the small **'a'** stands for. Wise activities can be boosted or undermined by the approach or attitude with which they are applied. Your attitude and approach greatly influences the amount of effort that you expend and the activities that you undertake. In turn this can helpfully or unhelpfully influence the results you can achieve. I have seen highly talented people consistently achieve mediocre results because of the attitude 'baggage' that they bring to work; of course the opposite is also true in that positive 'baggage' can be carried too! The professional salesperson creates and reinforces their own working context to maintain enthusiasm and energy. This is about setting out with a positive and determined attitude and consistently looking for opportunities. I am certainly not suggesting that you can be immune to difficulties and distractions; I am saying however that you can (apart from times of real crises or trauma) choose your focus and approach. You can choose to see what can be done as opposed to focussing on what cannot be done. You can choose to feel good about 'progress' rather than distraught about 'failure'.

In essence the formula is saying that your level of engagement can be seen as the sum of your effort, activities and results; multiplied by your attitude/approach. It is well worth you spending some time thinking about this because it has the ability to make a difference. In the next chapter I have developed a questionnaire that will certainly help you to objectively understand your levels of engagement.

Thought provokers

Here are some useful 'thought-provokers'. They relate to the application of an 'Engaged' mindset

Consider the analogy of the paddler, wader and swimmer. Which of the three best describes your level of engagement over the last 12 months?

What should you be thinking about and focussing on?

Consider the engagement level formula...

Engagement = $(E+A+R)a$.

If you had to rate your *'effort'* out of 10 — what rating would you give yourself?

If you had to rate your *'activities'* out of 10 — being very objective, what rating would you give yourself?

If you had to rate your *'results'* out of 10 — how would you score yourself?

If you had to rate your *'attitude'* out of 10 — what rating would you give yourself?

What actions do you think you should you take as a result of your thinking about the formula?

What is the difference between being fully engaged and being wisely engaged?

You can be fully engaged without doing so in a wise and considered manner. You cannot be wisely engaged without doing so in a fully engaged and totally committed manner. The point is...choose to have both!

Think about the above ratings as you go through the detail of Chapter 7.

7

A PRACTICAL MINDSET

In the previous chapter we noted the importance of having the right attitude and doing the right activities. We also saw the need to put in the appropriate amount of effort to get the desired results. We now look at the issue of 'activities' in a bit more detail by engaging in a self-assessment activity. It has been broken down into eight sections and primarily they are focussed on the appropriate activities that will get you the results that you need; it stands to reason that your focus and energy should be applied to them.

Please remember that self-evaluation must be a risk-free undertaking and that it should be interesting, challenging and helpfully intense. There is little point in engaging in a superficial and self-congratulatory internal dialogue; your goal is to fulfil your full potential and to do this you need to identify your full potential. This requires you to be brutally honest without being harshly critical; if you would be hesitant to say something to somebody else, because of the offence that they might take, then you should not say it to yourself. This is about an objective assessment and it is not at all a self-remonstration exercise. You often see sports personalities such as famous tennis players screaming at themselves and giving themselves a real telling off for missing a point or failing to return a service. This might work in sport but it certainly does not work in your world. You need to be objective and appropriately emotional. It is good news to find things that you are not doing as well as you could! It is an opportunity to improve your results, it is not a point of criticism.

I would strongly advise you not to skim over the questions but engage with them and look for significant discoveries. This activity is not about merely answering the questions but rather about looking to learn and seeking ways to be better.

Please rate how well you do the following…tick the ratings for each section and then read through the notes for that section. You might want to re-rate yourself following the notes to ensure that you develop an accurate assessment that you can work with.

Outlook and Approach

How well do you do the following?

		poor	ok	good	expert
1	You focus on winning all the available business from your territory – not just current customers				
2	You set out each day to look for and take advantage of all selling opportunities.				
3	You get excited about commercial opportunities and motivate yourself and others.				
4	You make full use of your trading day. It is packed with productive activities and sales visits.				

5	Your week is spent in a 'commercially wise' way. You major on actions that gain sales and build ongoing business.				

There are people out in the sales field who have settled into a comfortable routine with predictable days and consistent results. I fully understand the benefit of consistent results however it is important to ensure that consistency is not the goal; maximising sales is the goal. Q1 highlights the difference in approach between managing a territory and managing a customer base. Most sales roles require you to increase the number of customers that you have and not just deal with the current list. To lead and manage a territory you obviously have to consider your current customer base and look for ways to increase the range and the quantities. However you also have to think bigger than your current customers, you have to actively think about commercial opportunities and seek them out. An entrepreneurial approach often yields better results than a 'customer management' approach. Organic growth is highly valued and is certainly a significant goal to engage in; compound growth takes the organic build and adds significantly to it. Your ability to do this is highly valued by your organisation.

Q2 reinforces this thinking by asking you to consider your outlook and approach for each working day. If you set out to do something you are much more likely to see the opportunities to do it than if you did not have that in your mind in the first place.

This is about being proactive rather than reactive. If looking for all the commercial opportunities available actually becomes your **purpose** then it will trigger you to see **possibilities**. This is a valuable position to be in because if you can then see a wide range of possibilities, then you then have a good number of **choices** that you can make. Once you have made a good choice it becomes obvious that you can then develop the **tactics** that will deliver your goal. I would strongly recommend that you adopt this thought process and use it to develop helpful and wise tactics. Obviously the weaker the 'start' of the chain i.e. purpose then the weaker the whole chain. In summary it goes…

>…have a strong purpose
>…identify a range of possibilities
>…make wise choices
>…develop tactics.

Q3 provokes you to think about your levels of excitement. It is often easy to think back to those early days of your career when everything was an exciting challenge. You did not have 'problems' you just had successes that had not quite materialised yet. You probably had a sense of optimistic excitement that served like a 'firewall' to negativity. This is as natural as it is temporary for most people, it tends not to be sustainable in the long run unless it is maintained and nurtured. The 'slings and arrows' of outrageous customer demands will at some time prove too strong for optimism. This is when a sense of perspective and realism work well.

If you have crossed over from excitement for each day…to neutrality about each day do not simply accept that; decide to address your outlook and approach. If you are misfortunate enough to have crossed over from neutrality onto 'dread' for each day, do not hide this; confront it so that you can do something about it. It is something that happens to most of us at one time or another and it can be cyclical. If this is the case you might find it helpful to recalibrate your perspective about your job. I would suggest that 'neutrality' is a significant warning sign to look out for. It is when you don't feel any enthusiasm for doing something but on the other hand you don't mind if you have to do it. This is the early stages of demotivation and it should be seen as a serious symptom. It is when we simply accept this state that we start developing unhelpful outlooks and approaches; we think it is OK because it is not negative. Neutrality is the training ground for negativity and negativity is the force that de-skills you; it is necessary to feel strongly about success in order to make it happen.

You probably have the freedom and flexibility to choose your own tactics and how you spend your time. This is a privilege that many other jobs do not have. You have the opportunity to better yourself just by using your wits, experience and intelligence. You have the pleasure of interacting with many different people and building strong working relationships. These are good things to have and when we slip into a dull routine it is these things that we need to remind ourselves of. My advice for you if you do need a recalibration of your approach is to recognise the lessons from the 'YOU plc' analogy and determine to be the consummate professional. Decide to develop your skills and capabilities further.

Identify part of your role in which you could/should be acting at 'expert level' and plot a path to make it so. If you engage in and focus on excellence you tend to avoid dull routine. It is not a problem at all to experience temporary disillusionment, it is a huge problem if you decide to simply accept that as being your lot in life!

Q4 raises an important point about the use of your day. This is not about trying to get you to extend your hours and work harder; it is rather suggesting that you focus on productivity and carefully consider the return on the investment of your time. Old fashioned sales managers will go on about filling your day with as many sales interactions as you can and applaud attempts to race up and down your country to meet deadlines. In this modern digital world there will be many tasks that you can engage in to prepare for meetings, sell on-line, use social media and audit websites etc. – these are all a part of your selling process. The goal is to ensure that what you do can make a significant difference. The enemy of productivity is unquestioned routine and so it makes sense to take a hard and objective look at your routing, choices and activities. Obviously I am not talking about filling your day with just any meetings; you want to engage in well planned business interactions that have significant goals attached to them. The more of these types of interactions that you can have in a day then the higher your sales figures will be. Use the full day wisely so that you can switch off at the end of it.

Q5 again continues the theme and hints at the need to really focus on where you are going. Too often I talk to sales professionals who are calling on their customers because of a call cycle or to keep their visit rate up. This is not a helpful way to use up your precious time. I can think of one example where a customer was religiously visited every month but the account was 'on hold' from credit control all this time and no order could be taken. A useful way of thinking to assist this would be the question… "If I were on commission only…would I spend my time this way?" You would only do those things that make a difference and this thinking is consistent with the YOU plc model. 'Commission only' thinking is a useful way of provoking focus about the return on the investment of your time. This is an area that is continued below.

Business Acumen – make it your USP
(unique Sales Proposition)

How you answer these questions gives you a real insight into your own 'business acumen'. Acumen is all about the ability to make decisions based on good judgement. It points to wisdom, an acute awareness and an impressive mental agility; it encapsulates a sharpness and incisiveness of thinking. An individual known for their business acumen is someone who can make cunning, clever and brilliant business decisions. Such an approach maximises all opportunities and cunningly handles challenges and obstacles. Such an individual reads situations and events with an almost instinctive understanding of what is going to get a good result.

Is your planning and engagement in your market place an example of strong business acumen? Are your choices an example of a wise strategy driven with a purposeful zeal?

Planning

How well do you do the following?

		poor	ok	good	expert
6	You plan 'achievements' for each day and week.				
7	You get the most appropriate mix of time between driving and time with customers.				
8	Your week is planned and made up of powerful business meetings and events.				
9	Your meetings are scheduled and booked at least one week in advance.				
10	You monitor and respond to personal performance metrics and indicators of progress.				

There is a huge difference between planning your activities for the week and planning your 'achievements' for the week. The activities are about what you will do and how you will use up your time however achievements are what you expect to gain, win or deliver. Planned achievements should be the very reason that you are engaged in any activity in the first place and it is important that you get the order of thinking correct. It is not helpful to plan for an activity and only then question what you would like to achieve from it; this needs to happen the other way around. It is much wiser to clarify what you want to achieve and then decide what is the most helpful and appropriate way of getting. Q6 confirms the wisdom of doing this on both a daily and a weekly basis. Options for how you spend your day need to be very carefully considered. There is no definite right or wrong in this but some things will hinder progress and others will make it easier. There is a definite helpful and unhelpful and you should be on the lookout for any self-imposed inefficiencies.

Q7 provokes you to think about driving time. Some people tell me that they value driving time as it gives them an opportunity to catch-up on phone calls and think about the next meeting but most say that it can be lost time. I know people who do all of their administration first thing in the morning to avoid the rush hour in order to make their journey time as short as possible. Others park up towards the end of the day to write up reports and deal with emails so that they let the worst of rush hour pass before they start the journey. There is great benefit in planning customer visits carefully, taking advantage of clusters of customers and the use of overnight stays. There is a balance to be struck and it is a personal one because each of us has very different personal situations. However you currently choose to do it you will need to regularly review it and be prepared to question it. You should not be offended if your sales manager provokes you to think about it further. Call plans that were developed some time ago may well be out of date as new customers are won, priorities shift and opportunities arise. It needs to be a carefully considered choice rather than a well used routine. You might find it helpful to have a colleague sense–check it for you. There is always value in having your time management looked at through a different set of eyes.

Q8 continues the theme but from a slightly different perspective. It points to the difference between a customer visit and a powerful business meeting. The difference is often all about intention and preparation. This should not be driven by your customer's expectations but rather by your ambitions and your sense of personal professionalism. Some customers are vey happy with an informal chat and like to talk about products and 'things' in a very general way whilst others are very much wanting to 'get down to business' and get the meeting moving on quickly. You can flex to your customer's style without compromising your commercial imperatives. Style is all about how you interact whereas focus is all about the reasons why you want to have the interaction. Change your style but don't change your focus unless there is a very good reason to do so. Adapting to a customer's preferences is not the same as conceding to them. This is all about being flexible and agile whilst still keeping control and maintaining the initiative. The definition of what a powerful meeting actually is should be all about the way you or your organisation defines it rather than how the customer sees it. I find it interesting when talking to customers of my clients when they readily point out who the 'good' sales reps are; they actually mean 'good' from their perspective and what suits them as customers. This might be someone who has loads of information and good promotional ideas however it can also be because they are not demanding and act in a customer service way rather than a sales way. Whilst there is a great overlap between what your organisation wants and what your customer wants…there can often be a significant gap and as per chapter 4 it is wise to remember who *your* customer actually is.

The issue of planned meetings is raised in Q9 and this means different things to different people. Best practice involves having meetings that are scheduled, with purpose driven agendas and specific outcomes. It is not just that they are in the diary and confirmed...it is that they are prepared for. If, for some inexplicable reason, you decided only to invest in one area of your performance this year I would suggest that planning for meetings would be a good choice to make; one that would pay good dividends. Improvisation works well for comedy shows...it does not work for professional business meetings.

In chapter 4 we looked at issues of indicators of progress. If you were a business you would want to measure the key areas that give you insight into how well you are doing and the progress that you are making. Q10 points to this and it is a significant area of opportunity for many people. The old adage is true... 'what gets measured gets attention' and the more of your activities that you measure the more you are able to improve efficiency and productivity. It is important to remember that just because something cannot be measured accurately as a metric, it does not mean that it should not be measured at all.

There are a number of metrics that you should consider and these are listed below. I have not listed the 'givens' of sales results and comparisons to target and last year.

- Number of business meetings per week. This provides you with an understanding of the opportunities for business that you have created and taken advantage of.

- Sales revenue to business meetings ratio. This will give you a weekly 'average sale value' which helps you to track progress and identify trends.
- Hours driving to hours in meetings ratio. This may provoke a determination to look for efficiencies and recheck the assumptions in your route planning.
- Hours planning to hours in meetings ratio. This gives you an understanding of the time taken to be in a position of maximum influence. You may find that less meeting time and more planning time will give you a better overall sales result. It may indicate that you are not spending much time at all on this vital activity.
- Time spent pie chart. This involves creating a weekly or monthly pie chart of the main uses of your time. What percentage is given to driving, planning, meetings and 'other' tasks such as admin? Does this reflect the behaviour and choices of a purpose driven and highly efficient sales professional?
- Number of endorsees gained. Within the organisations that you sell to there are probably those that are firm endorsees (i.e. they are happy to endorse you to others) and there will also be those you are politely neutral or mildly positive. It makes a lot of sense to create more endorsees so that you can win over the very people who will win over others in their organisation. If you count how many you gain in a month or quarter, it will focus your mind on it. This is an opportunity to grow your 'relationship assets' so that you have more influence within each customer's organisation.

The very fact that you spend some time capturing such information means that it will influence your choices and behaviour. This in turn will have an impact on your success.

Meeting preparation

How well do you do the following?

		poor	ok	good	expert
11	You have a thorough understanding of and insight into your customer's business.				
12	You know who the decision shares and makers are and what drives them.				
13	You have a clear and written goal for what products/services you want to sell for each meeting.				
14	You have a clear and written goals for business development for each meeting.				
15	You have a relationship with key decision shapers and makers for your customers.				

Preparation is the next logical step to planning and this section focuses on your engagement in the activities that set you up for success. It is a 'given' that you know your own business together with its strengths and selling points. It is naturally accepted that you thoroughly understand the features and benefits of your product range and that specific 'points of persuasion' are second nature to you. These are not enough however and Q11 and Q12 provoke you to think about things from your customer's perspective.

See what your customers see

Are you in a position to understand the challenges that your customers face and the difficulties that they have to overcome? Can you see this from an individual and organisational perspective? Do you have insight into the working world of the person that you are meeting? Such insight would mean an understanding of their personal drivers of behaviour as well as the rules and practices that they have to abide by. Do you have a wide 'sphere of influence' within your customer's organisation that empowers you and enables you to influence thinking and decisions? This is about having trusted contacts and relationships at all levels and across as many functions as possible. In my experience these are very important questions and are trains of thought that the experts take very seriously. In order to successfully persuade people you have to understand them. In order to understand them you have to have interaction and relationship with them. To do this you have to work hard to create opportunities and see the bigger organisational picture. If you can gain allies and friends in their organisation you will be able to have helpful influence. It should be said however that if you do benefit from such good and wide relationships then you should value them highly. They should be nurtured as opposed to being on the end of a 'hard-sell'. In order to influence an organisation you have to be able to accurately and insightfully relate to people within it. Remember the 'business model' thinking that was explained in chapter 4? This is where it pays dividends for you; it is the way that you understand how you can assist and be of value to your customer. In order for you to stand out in the crowd of eager and enthusiastic sales professionals you need to have and display an insight into what is important and valued in the organisation that you are selling to. This enables you to identify ways that you can you be a real help and be a positive influence on what they are trying to do. An important question to ask and then answer is... *"How can your products/services enrich their business and make them more successful?"* To enrich something is to make it more valuable and more desired. It literally makes it different by transferring value to it.

In most businesses there are the decision 'shapers', the decision 'makers' and the decision 'ratifiers' and it is important to recognise their different roles and understand the drivers that shape their decisions and choices.

The *decision shapers* are people whose expertise and knowledge is highly valued. They have an experience that is widely respected and when they offer an opinion it is taken very seriously; it is a brave manager that contradicts them. Such people greatly influence the buying choices of their organisations and they need to be treated as subject matter experts. This involves giving due respect and consulting them. The more influence you have with these individuals the more influence you have with the business.

The *decision makers* are typically the professional buyers and they have responsibility for making wise and appropriate choices. Each decision is a personal risk as well as a risk to their organisation. The risk is personal because their credibility and professional reputation is directly linked to the success of the decisions that they make. If you can be a trusted source of wisdom to enable them to make good decisions then you will be valued and you will never struggle to get meetings. If you are seen as someone going through the motions to 'flog' products then you end up being more of a threat to their success than an assistance; this will obviously not help! Of course there is no sense in being neutral either because in actual fact, if you are not a help to them then you are a hindrance.

Decision Ratifiers are those who sense-check and approve the decisions of others. They tend not to give out orders but are certainly in a position to say 'no' to them. They might be senior buyers who have a bigger purchase picture on their mind. They may be involved in strategic decisions that are not yet known to the buyers. They may also be senior financial people who have the bigger financial picture in mind and have the authority to demand that decisions are made for reasons other than what the buyers are measured on; an example of this is cash flow constraints. Managing Directors may also fit the ratifier role as they may make the same observations and decisions above but may also know some of the strategic changes and opportunities that their business is about to engage it. Of course all three of the above can also become absolute endorsees but to do this they may need to interact with someone like you.

They need you to persuade them to see things differently and make positive choices. You need to know people and be known to them; this reinforces the importance of your 'sphere of influence'; the wider and deeper it is then the more influence you have in an organisation. It is a real weakness to rely on just one or two people because you have then made them into 'single points of failure' i.e. if they leave or cannot influence in any way then you are lost. It goes without saying that you may not be in any position to get to know the managing director and all of the others that you would like to influence. It is important to understand the principle of this and to apply it to your working world.

A purpose driven mindset

Q13-15 draw your attention to the specific goals that you set for meetings. This is one of the most important factors that influences your success and it therefore warrants close attention. If you have a strong 'purpose' then you will find it easier to muster and coordinate all of your resources, capabilities and energy in order to meet that purpose. If you do not have a strong purpose (set of goals) you will not push yourself to improve or be creative to excel.

As a sales professional you should always have three categories of goals for every sales interaction that you facilitate and these include…

Product Sales Goals. This is a note of the specific products/services that you intend to sell. It is not a prediction of what they are likely to buy it is rather a note of your intentions. To make this measurable you would probably include dates and amounts. You know that your proposal and presentation must have a persuasive and compelling justification for making such a decision. It is not a failure if you do not manage to achieve these goals; it is a failure if you do not set an aspirational goal that stretches your capability and ensures that you do the appropriate amount of preparation.

Business Development Goals. As a business professional you have a sales mindset that looks beyond the current interaction and is focused on extracting all the available business from that customer. With that in mind you know the importance of developing future business and expanding your range in terms of volume, depth and width of take-up. You need to be aware of the trends and plans of your customer's business so that you can see the appropriate opportunities. This means you having specific goals for each of the sales interactions that you engage in. If you were selling to a retailer this might include winning new space on their sales floor, prime positions and window displays. It could include winning prime positions on websites and creating in-store endorsees for your products. It would definitely include setting up joint promotions and events. These are the goals that you have for your meetings; you sell an idea, convert it into a concept and then get approval for the plan.

Business Relationship Goals. You need to have good working relationships with different people and at different levels. You need to know the decision makers, shapers and ratifiers. It will be helpful if you have a working relationship with the people who are in the decision chain. It will be very helpful to your commercial strategy to have goals about business relationships. Have in mind the people that you want to meet, get to know better, influence and be influenced by.

The purpose of a goal is to establish your focus, inspire you to extra effort and measure the success of your activities. Good goals trigger good performance.

Leading Meetings

How well do you do the following?

		poor	ok	good	expert
16	Do you have a clear meeting strategy that takes a logical approach to meeting your goals?				
17	Do you talk through your agenda and 'prime' people for a productive meeting?				
18	Do you manage time during the meeting ensuring that it is productively spent…and that you cover all you need to in the available opportunity?				

19	Do you 'wrap up' the meeting when it is appropriate? Do you skilfully draw it to a close, summarising the main issues and confirming any action points?				
20	Do you end with pleasantries and agree a date for the next meeting – including what could be covered?				

Just to reinforce a point made earlier on, we are not talking about sales visits or sales calls; each interaction should be a planned meeting. The idea of a visit or a 'pop in' call has no place in the mindset of a professional sales person. You will note that I always refer to 'meetings' in this book; these may last for 10 minutes or for 3 hours – they are a structured opportunity to persuade people to make decisions and take actions. Meetings will be a constant in your working world and it makes sense to become a subject matter expert at them. To assist people to become such an expert I have published a book that can be found on Amazon entitled "Meetings That Make A Difference" – it has over 100 tips that you can apply immediately.

There is a very big difference between attending meetings, facilitating meetings and leading them. Yes, they all involve you being there but the contribution that you make differs greatly. If you set out to be a business professional and take your career and success seriously you will never simply 'attend' meetings. You always see such events as an opportunity to learn and develop. You see the chance to make contacts and have influence. You note the responsibility to use your time wisely and invest it well. You cannot always choose which meetings you have to attend but you can always choose your particular approach and contribution to them. You can choose your attitude and you can choose the value and significance of your attendance. Of course this is different to facilitating big meetings when you have the opportunity to skilfully lead people into pooling their skills, knowledge and insight. In this part of the questionnaire however we are referring to leading meetings; to taking the lead.

Successful salespeople fully respect a corporate hierarchy but are never bound by it. You should make the choice to fully understand the organisational structure and levels of seniority of the people that you are meeting and then use what you discover wisely. This demands conscious courtesy and a genuine respect; it is an engagement with people on a professional-to-professional basis.

All of this means that you want to lead meetings and Q16 points to the need for a strategy, a series of steps that will lead you to a desired end point. Yet again we see the importance of 'goals' because the very first part of developing a compelling strategy is to know what you want to achieve! Your strategy is simply the logical sequence of steps that will get you to where you want to be.

Meeting Tactics

When developing your strategy it is helpful to think of the tactics available to you and I always recommend choosing one or more of the following…

1. **Inform & Advise**. This is when you want to present information and share insight. You are passing on information that will help them in their working world. You will find it useful to be clear about 'what will be covered', 'why it is relevant' to cover it and 'what to do' with their new found knowledge.

2. **Discuss & Explore**. This is when you want to engage your customer thinking about things and to capture their views and perspectives. You obviously have an end goal in mind however sometimes a thorough discussion is needed for customers to really understand the benefits and wisdom of your proposal. This should be about listening and not seeing their points as objections but as genuine points of view. Your customers 'framing' of products and situations is definitely influencing their choices so you had better be able to relate to it.

3. **Debate & Evaluate.** Sometimes you have to debate the merits of a proposition because you see it differently. I chose my words carefully and did not frame this in a conflict context; it is better not to disagree on something but rather debate the merits in an attempt to influence each other. This stops it being personal so that nobody has to 'back down' if they choose to change their mind. If you help a customer evaluate a proposal then you can influence the points that make up the

evaluation.

4. **Decide & Close.** Sometimes in a meeting you have to bring things to a conclusion because 'decision avoidance' is the oldest trick in the book for those who struggle to say 'no thanks'. You might want to use an agenda point to trigger a decision point (closing).

5. **Create & Innovate.** There are also times when you might want to use a part of a meeting or an agenda point to think differently with your customer and work together to innovate and think out of the box. This is a tremendous opportunity to be able to be directly and uniquely relevant to your customer and develop solutions that your competitors will not be aware of. Be sure to communicate this as a conscious strategy rather than a response to not knowing what to do next.

6. **Inspire and Energise.** This is when you become a source of positive energy and a 'breath of fresh air' to your customers. This is when you take the time to provide your customer with positive feedback and to point out some of their successes and wins. You can demonstrate admiration for certain achievements or activities and you can infect them with your enthusiasm and energy. This agenda point can inspire them to see beyond the challenges and recognise the opportunities of certain positions, markets and activities. People like to be around people who can do this and they will always welcome your visit to their premises as well as take your phone calls.

7. **Warn & Caution.** There are also times when it is

appropriate to use an agenda point as a 'warn and caution' opportunity. It is when you helpfully point out the pitfalls of certain approaches or the downside of not taking a particular course of action. This should not be confused with the 'distress close' when you imply an unwanted effect of not making a decision e.g. "I only have 3 in stock and I cannot guarantee having any available for you next week". This is more about genuinely providing insight that enables them to take an alternative viewpoint and plot a different course to avoid pitfalls.

In Q17 the concept of 'priming' is introduced and this is a very helpful skill for you to master. So much of human behaviour is a result of people being 'primed' to act in a certain way. Essentially this refers to a particular stimulus (words, pictures, smells etc.) that triggers an expected later response. By way of an example imagine if I showed you three pictures; they were of a baboon, an orangutan and a chimpanzee. If I then asked you to tell me the first 'fruit' that comes into your mind, you would most probably say 'banana'. You could have carefully thought about every fruit that you know. You could have thought about which fruits you like most of all. However the images that I showed you have stayed in your mind and as a result of the question you have 'linked' the pictures to the fruit request. It does not always work however I am sure that you get the point. You have actually been 'primed' to say banana. You have not in any way been manipulated; the natural thinking process has just been used to trigger a likely response. How does this apply to leading meetings? Very simply you can send an agenda that primes your customer to look forward to your meeting or to dread it. You can prime them to see the value of your interaction in advance or you can hope that they get the point when you meet. Essentially this is all about positively managing the expectations of your customer so that you can meet them. You have the opportunity to send an agenda in advance and if you do be very aware of the difference between an agenda point and a thought-provoking primer.

You might suggest that agenda point 1 for the sales interaction/meeting is 'Product XYZ'. This actually tells your customer very little. It leaves them to be led by their assumptions of how useful this will be rather than your priming of how useful this subject will be. In effect you are allowing their cumulative experience of meetings with sales reps to set the benchmark of how useful this meeting will be. If instead your agenda point 1 is "The 5 ways that Product XYZ will grow your business this year" then you will have their attention because they see the personal value. This is an important sales principle; when preparing for sales interactions and when communicating your agenda don't just inform - be persuasive and provoke thought.

Q18-20 provoke you to think about the wise use of time and the need to skilfully draw things to a close. The rookie rep thinks that the longer a meeting goes on for, the more successful it will be. Both you and your customer have time pressures and you are both very conscious that you need a good 'return' on the investment of your time. This means that you will have a limited period with your customer so you have to engage in wise planning to make the most of it.

However you may have noticed that some customers are not as keen as you are to get to the main selling points or the well thought through demonstration. They can be happy to talk about generalities and talk in detail about the things that really interest them – without an eye on the clock. It is you who needs to be very aware of how much time you have, what you need to cover and how well the meeting is following your plan.

You need to 'wrap up' things at some point and a good way of doing this is to summarise the main issues that have been discussed as well as confirming any action points agreed. This wrapping up signifies the end to the meeting. You will have been 'closing' all way through (we will cover this later) and this is a good time to confirm quantities and perhaps push for a little more if appropriate. It is always helpful at this time to set a date for the next meeting but this varies from industry to industry – the point is that even if it is not appropriate to plan the next date, you definitely can prime them to look forward to it and see the value of it.

Participating in meetings

How well do you do the following?

		poor	ok	good	expert
21	Do you listen carefully during meetings - taking notes and asking questions to clarify your understanding?				

22	Do you give a considered and careful response to questions, queries and objections – seeing them as a part of the selling process?				
23	Do you ensure that you fully understand their viewpoint and why they have it – before providing a counter argument?				
24	Do your customers see you as someone who they can engage with commercially…a fellow business person to discuss and debate opportunities with?				
25	Do you communicate genuine courtesy and respect to the people you are meeting with?				

Q21-25 are self explanatory and provoke you to think about the way that you influence the dynamics of your sales interaction. It is all about the opportunities that you have to create, reinforce and nurture a helpful and appropriate environment. If it is obvious that you are listening closely to what they have to say then you will mostly find that your attention is reciprocated. If you want to influence someone and persuade them to take a course of action it is vital to thoroughly understand all that they have to say and gain good insight into why they are saying it. As I stated in an earlier chapter you have to understand someone if you want to influence them.

One of the common pitfalls of the over enthusiastic amateur is that they don't actually listen to what the other person is trying to communicate, they just listen to what is being said so that they can formulate counter arguments. Effective selling that creates lifelong customers is not a duelling or sparring activity. You can easily win an argument whilst losing a sale; sales revenue is much more valuable than a memory full of successful arguments. It is also wise to think about the difference between 'hearing' and 'listening' to what is being said. Hearing is all about capturing the words that are being used and understanding the direct meaning of them. Listening takes this one step further and it provokes you to empathise, wonder what is triggering their approach and even think through the ramifications of it; all whist the person is talking. This is what is referred to in Q22 about giving a considered and careful response to questions, queries and objections. You have to have listened carefully to do this well.

Q24 is designed to assist you to think about the impression that you are giving and how helpful it actually is. Different customers will probably value different things in their relationship with you and it is important that you present yourself appropriately and 'be' the sort of person that they would like to work with. Remember that your relationship is strictly business when you are engaged in your job and you need to be seen as a fellow 'business person'; this will give you a wider sphere of influence. It is understandable and even common for sales people to become friendly with their long standing customers and for strong friendships to emerge. If this is the case it is important that you discuss when you are in 'friend' mode and when you are in 'business' mode. There may well be some blurring of the position however it is important that they can say 'no thanks' without it affecting the relationship and that you can also say 'I have to give this great deal to the highest bidder' (which may not be your friend). If you experience an awkwardness then you should really discuss it because such things tend not to be self-healing and you run the risk of losing a good customer as well as a friend. Generally speaking, in a sales environment, it is wise to keep personal relationships and business relationships separate.

Do you have a wide reputation for being a courteous and respectful person to interact with? If you found yourself hesitating to answer that question then you might have discovered another opportunity to be even better. Q25 asks you this because the immediate answer should be an immediate and emphatic 'yes' however this is not always the case. It is obviously right to have respect and courtesy for your main contacts and the people around them however it can also be very helpful to be liked by a wider audience. Giving respect often triggers a reciprocal response.

Presenting products and solutions

How well do you do the following?

		poor	ok	good	expert
26	Do you support your selling propositions with well thought out and compelling 'reasons to buy'?				

27	Do you have a structured approach…not leading with your best points…building up to your best points?				
28	Do you 'test the water' or 'trial close' during your presentation?				
29	Do you pass on useful tips, hints and techniques to sales people to help them 'sell through' all the products?				
30	Do you provide useful and relevant advice about displaying and merchandising the products?				

This section of the self-assessment exercise encourages you to think about the way you present your products/services to people. I would suggest that this is both an issue and an opportunity for all professional sales people and possibly even more so for the seasoned professional. As mentioned in an earlier chapter the ease with which we can all go onto 'auto-pilot' is frankly frightening. As soon as we stop thinking about what we are doing and consciously considering our choices we start compromising; we begin achieving consistency not excellence.

This topic is obviously included in books about sales techniques and whilst this text is more about a sales 'mindset' I must make some comment about techniques. There are some fundamental elements of the selling process that are universal to all products and apply in all countries; 'presenting products' is one of those. Consider the following basics about this topic and when they are standard practice you can move on to advanced techniques.

Without a structured 'proposition' or sales story you are not really selling, you are just talking. Your proposition is your reasoned argument; it should be persuasive and comprehensive. Your whole interaction should be delivering a relevant and compelling recommendation; a plan that provides them with the benefits and outcomes that they need. It should be seen as a considered recommendation that warrants serious consideration and a considered response. Whilst there may be much involved in the overall pitch you should be able to summarise it in a sentence or two and then be able to elaborate on it. Propositions should also have a 'call to action' – what is it that you want people to do next?

The concept of 'reasons to buy' is a very important one. Too often customers receive masses of information as if the information alone triggers a decision. I am always struck by the fact that 'data' does not seem to trigger decisions or engagement from people. By way of an example we all know the data about cigarettes; smoking kills you...you will definitely die earlier than you would if you did not smoke. This is widely accepted, it is an absolute fact however it does not deter many people from smoking. One theory for this is it is because people have not personalised the data and considered the ramifications of it personally or for those around them. It is when the data becomes 'personal' that it becomes influential. This is what I mean about real 'reasons to buy' – it is when you convert helpful product/service information into compelling and personal reasons to make a choice or decision.

It is best not to lead with your killer selling point. Present a foundation of your premise, build it up with relevant points and then employ your killer argument. Trial Closing must be a standard activity. This simply involves checking your understanding as you go along and 'bagging' any decisions that have been made. By decisions I refer to the 'narrowing down' process during your discussion. You might establish that the customer has a preference for range 'A' over range 'B' and this determines the rest of your conversation. You determine this by 'trial closing' in a way that is so subtle that it is not noticeable.

If you are selling to businesses that will in turn be selling the products on again, it is imperative that your presentation includes selling points that they can use. In this case you want to major on the principle of 'sales-through' i.e. you help them to sell the products on. This might be through joint promotions, events, display materials or joint presentations.

Closing the sale

How well do you do the following?

		poor	ok	good	expert
31	Do you recognise the 'signs' that it is time to stop presenting and start provoking a decision?				
32	Do you recognise 'buying signals' that are given out?				
33	Do you know a number of recognised 'closing techniques' to use at different times with different people?				

34	Do you directly/indirectly ask the customer if they would like to buy?				
35	Do you recommend 'add on' appropriate products or services to maximise the value of the sale? Do you encourage a decision to buy these as well?				

Again this is a topic for sales technique books however I would like to take this opportunity to confirm some helpful tips, hints and techniques.

Q31-32 provoke you to be aware of the signals that are given out. This requires you to be alert for the subtle shifts in the environment, the atmosphere and responses your customer provides. I mentioned earlier that time is a valuable commodity to everyone involved; you both know that there will be a specific point when the value of the interaction starts dropping and it is time to wrap things up. I know some sales professionals who feel obligated to use every minute that is made available to them and I would caution against that. You need to have a reputation for conducting useful and relevant sales proposals and that time spent with you is interesting and helpful. This means that you should judge the length of the meeting according to a balance of what you set out to achieve and what your customer would find useful. The first sign that you should shift from presenting and move onto closing is when you have completed a persuasive and compelling proposal; don't keep talking, go quiet and encourage a response.

Another indicator is that your customer's attention visibly dissipates, they are no longer intently listening and have changed to politely listening. This will certainly affect your ability to influence them and if you wait too long you may lose the gains that you have already made. You will have been looking for visual clues as you have been discussing and presenting and the main indicator that you are looking for is when the focus shifts from discussion about the validity of the proposal onto discussion about the implementation of it. This could be subtle however it is an important point of the interaction because you want to lock in a decision as early as possible. A discussion about logistics before a decision will always be harder than a discussion about logistics after a decision to buy has been made. It is time to 'close'.

Q33 asks you to think about the closing process and to specifically consider the different techniques that you can use. A tennis player may have a formidable serving technique that they use to great advantage. If their 'serve returning' technique is poor however they are going to have limited success. The same principle applies to the whole of the selling process and especially to closing. Of the wide choice of established options there are at least four foundational techniques that you should be fluent with…

Direct Close. Quite simply this is exactly what it implies. You directly ask them if they would like to proceed. "Shall we go ahead with that?" or "would you like to put them on order" are examples of this approach. It all sounds so simple however there is one factor that can really limit a sales person's willingness to directly close the sale. It is about a fear of rejection or fear of a straight 'no thanks'. A 'no thanks' is not a rejection…it is a helpful clarification of where you are and what you need to do next. It is not a rejection of you or your proposal it is a clear statement that they are 'unsold'. The proposition has not hit home, the benefits of your offer are not compelling or there are key barriers that have not been overcome. It is better to know this than to hope it is not the case!

Alternative Close. Rather than creating a 'yes or no' situation this technique has you offering a alternative. It is inviting you to make a choice between two options and often people find this a lot more comfortable and sometimes they even appreciate the help to make a decision. It is about guiding them to their final choice. "Do you prefer the green or the red option?" or "Which of the two do you think would be most suitable" are examples of this approach.

Summary Close. This is an option that can actually be used with some of the others and it involves you listing (in reverse order of significance) the main benefits that you think have impacted your customer. You are summarising all of the key points and finishing off with the main sales point. It is a 'close' because you then go quiet. You have presented a persuasive list and now the onus is on the customer to respond.

Assumptive Close. Again this is self explanatory however this approach differs from the others in that you don't actually trigger a decision point, you just assume that one has been made. Obviously you have to earn the right to do this and you earn the right by excelling in all of the things that we have spoken about in this chapter. You might simply move on to talking about delivery options or even add-on selling items.

Continuous improvement

How well do you do the following?

		poor	ok	good	expert
36	Do you take the time after a meeting to write up some useful notes?				
37	Do you take the time to reflect on the meeting and identify the things that *you did well?*				
38	Do you take the time to reflect on the meeting and identify the things that *did not go so well* – and understand why?				
39	Do you take the time to reflect on the meeting and identify the things that *you would do differently next time?*				
40	Do you learn from your meetings and customer interactions?				

You have the opportunity to convert day-to-day work into a powerful learning experience and you do this by applying the principles outlined in Q36-40.

During a sales interaction there are quite literally

billions of stimuli impacting and influencing you and it should be a thoroughly engaging but tiring experience. You simply cannot remember everything and it is vital that you give your brain a rest and capture some important notes on either paper or a digital system. I talk about giving your brain a rest because it is very hard work remembering things and if you have a good note taking system then you can apply your mental energy to other things. Your organisation will most likely have a formal reporting system and I would encourage you to look beyond its flaws and use it the best you can. I have yet to hear a sales person extolling the benefits of their organisation's sales reporting process – they are all flawed. Wise people extract the best that they can from it and then supplement it with their own note-taking process.

You want to discover ways of self-coaching and ensuring that you gain experience and expertise from each business meeting. Q38-40 triggers you to think about the way that you do this and introduces a powerful but simple coaching activity that you can immediately use to create learning experiences. It is called the '3 Review Questions' model. This technique creates a thought process that engages you in continuous improvement. The questions are...

1. What worked well?
2. What did not work so well?
3. What would I do differently next time?

The reason for starting off with *'What worked well?'* is because it provides an opportunity to reinforce good practice, helpful activities and admirable efforts. It is too easy to think about what went wrong as opposed to what could have been better and this hinders your engagement in discovery; it can convert a useful learning experience into a risk of criticism. You never know in advance which of the three questions is going to be the most helpful to you; if you really knew the answers in advance you would not need to ask the questions!

Recognising what you have done well earns you the right to point out what you have not done well; it is this activity that separates a 'fair' self appraisal from the 'critical' self appraisal. Some useful questions that will help keep the focus on 'what worked well?' include...

- 'What were the signs that things were going well?'
- 'At what point were you sure that you had really been understood?'
- 'It sounds as if they had some very tough questions...what helped you or enabled you to have such good answers?'
- 'What do you think made that difference? 'Why do you think they relaxed at that point?'
- 'You feel the discussion started well...what do you think they were thinking at that point?'

I chose my words carefully when asking the second question; *'What did not work so well?'* It is intended to comfortably and honestly think through things without getting critical or looking for blame. The issue is not about 'what I did wrong' – you simply want to understand why it did not go the way you wanted it to so that you can extract learning points. There may be a wide variety of reasons and you have to look at all the options and consider everything.

The third question asks, *What would I do differently next time?'* It is a vital question that should still be asked even if things went brilliantly. You want to learn from every experience and then prepare for continued or even improved results.

Suggested Activities

Self evaluation is a very powerful process if used wisely and consistently. This checklist is a useful tool that you can use to identify ways to be even better. I would suggest the following activities...

- In chapter 9 there is a blank template of the checklist, photocopy it and go through it carefully, line by line. Evaluate yourself in an objective and honest way so that you can identify key areas for improvement.

- Identify some key areas for improvement and identify practical steps that you can take to improve.

- Read through this section of the book regularly until you are sure that you are excelling in each area...then commence reading books about specific sales techniques.

Jonathan Frost

8

A SUMMARY OF THE TIPS HINTS AND TECHNIQUES

I stated at the very beginning that this book is for those who spend their working life influencing people. It is for those of us who are engaged in selling products, services, ideas and opportunities; those that have to influence the choices and actions of others. A significant number of tips, hints and techniques have been provided and this chapter sets out to summarise them. It forms a useful 'go to' reference to access some of the key learning and it can also be used as a development plan to stimulate progress.

In Chapter 1 the focus was on providing a strong and clear definition of what selling actually is. It was noted that your personal definition of what selling is (conscious or unconscious) directly drives your performance and it is the stimulus that triggers your thinking and activity at work. You were encouraged to adopt the definition below.

Selling is the process of persuading people to make decisions and take actions.

We noted that there are four key elements to this definition; a) it is a process, b) it requires persuasion, c) it provokes decisions and d) it triggers specific actions. Without the 'persuasion factor' it is not actually selling.

In Chapter 2 the focus was on Sales Management. This is relevant even if this is not your job title because you are responsible for managing your career and the growth in your capability.

Chapter 3 introduced the concept of the Sales Mindset and noted 5 key elements. Your mind is 'set' in the way it sees, perceives and interpret things. This means that your approach to things will be consistent and that you are not overwhelmed by every single possibility when you are confronted with a situation or event. You see it and approach it according to your 'set' patterns.

A mindset is to the mind what sunglasses are to the eyes i.e. a filter that changes the appearance of everything. It does not change the things themselves, just how they look to you personally. Remember that nobody else benefits from your sunglasses; they only change the way that things look to you. So it is with your mindset; it makes sense of things and provides you with context...but it may well be different for others.

The 5 key elements of a helpful and powerful sales mindset are noted below and they are all about focus...

1. Focus on Focus
2. Focus on Professionalism
3. Focus on Persuasion (selling)
4. Focus on Opportunities
5. Focus on Technique

We noted that it is wise to frequently re-calibrate your mindset to make sure that it is relevant and wise in a changing work environment. Focus was defined as 'concentrated attention' and an essential skill to have. A 6 point checklist was provided and you were encouraged to helpfully evaluate yourself against them...

1. The professional is distinctly uncomfortable in any 'comfort zone'. They feel that if they are not stretching themselves then they are becoming stiff and inflexible.
2. They value their agility and their flexibility and recognise that they have to have new experiences to develop further. They actively look for and create situations that will enable this.
3. Professionals are self-driven with an urge to improve their skills, expand their knowledge and develop further capability. It is a sacrosanct imperative for them and it gives them the ability to convert day-to-day work into learning experiences.
4. They take notes during meetings and afterwards they take time out to consider what went well, what did not go so well and what they would do differently if they had that interaction over again.
5. The professional recognises that they need to develop a wide range of selling techniques that cover all of the stages of the selling process. They

know that they need to be skilled in the application of good techniques.

6. The professional is not content with the concept of 'good performance'...they see the need to convert 'good' into 'exceptional'.

Chapter 4 introduced the **YOU plc** analogy which encouraged you to think about yourself as if you were a business and not just as an employee. The first step would be to develop a business model and a helpful suggestion was provided...

To develop a powerful capability that others value highly and are prepared to pay for.

- You would need to have a valued product range that was consistently updated and refreshed (your skills, knowledge and expertise)
- You would need to provide an in-demand service (your ability to persuade people to make decisions and take actions)
- You would need to engage in commercial transactions (exchanging your capability for money)

You were encouraged to answer three extremely important questions...

- 'In what way have your skills been developed and enriched over the last 12 months?'
- 'In what way has your knowledge increased and become more valuable in the last 12 months?'
- 'In what areas have you established yourself as an expert at over the last year?'

Chapter 5 introduced the concept of Added-Value through the 'Two Fish Story'. Remember that you are always either adding value or taking value away. Your interactions are seldom neutral.

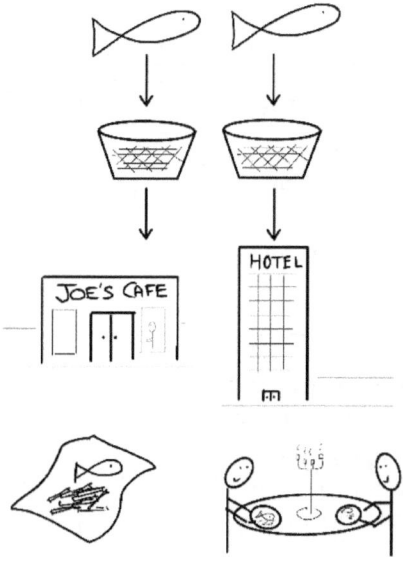

In Chapter 6 we discussed the 'Engaged Mindset' and noted that this was all about full participation and involvement. A formula for engagement was provided...

Engagement level = (E+A+R)a

E = Effort   A = Activities   R = Results   a = Attitude & Approach

In Chapter 7 a helpful self-assessment tool was presented which listed 40 thought-provoking and important questions. You were asked to rate how well you were doing and then read the text.

Outlook and Approach

		poor	ok	good	expert
1	You focus on winning all the available business from your territory – not just current customers				
2	You set out each day to look for and take advantage of all selling opportunities.				
3	You get excited about commercial opportunities and motivate yourself and others.				
4	You make full use of your trading day. It is packed with productive activities and sales visits.				
5	Your week is spent in a 'commercially wise' way. You major on actions that gain sales and build ongoing business.				

Planning

		poor	ok	good	expert
6	You plan 'achievements' for each day and week.				
7	You get the most appropriate mix of time between driving and time with customers.				
8	Your week is planned and made up of powerful business meetings and events.				
9	Your meetings are scheduled and booked at least one week in advance.				
10	You monitor and respond to personal performance metrics and indicators of progress.				

Meeting preparation

		poor	ok	good	expert
11	You have a thorough understanding of and insight into your customer's business.				
12	You know who the decision shares and makers are and what drives them.				
13	You have a clear and written goal for what products/services you want to sell for each meeting.				
14	You have a clear and written goals for business development for each meeting.				

15	You have a relationship with key decision shapers and makers for your customers.				

Leading Meetings

		poor	ok	good	expert
16	Do you have a clear meeting strategy that takes a logical approach to meeting your goals?				
17	Do you talk through your agenda and 'prime' people for a productive meeting?				
18	Do you manage time during the meeting ensuring that it is productively spent…and that you cover all you need to in the available opportunity?				
19	Do you 'wrap up' the meeting when it is appropriate? Do you skilfully draw it to a close, summarising the main issues and confirming any action points?				
20	Do you end with pleasantries and agree a date for the next meeting – including what could be covered?				

Participating in meetings

		poor	ok	good	expert
21	Do you listen carefully during meetings - taking notes and asking questions to clarify your understanding?				
22	Do you give a considered and careful response to questions, queries and objections – seeing them as a part of the selling process?				
23	Do you ensure that you fully understand their viewpoint and why they have it – before providing a counter argument?				
24	Do your customers see you as someone who they can engage with commercially…a fellow business person to discuss and debate opportunities with?				
25	Do you communicate genuine courtesy and respect to the people you are meeting with?				

Presenting products and solutions

		poor	ok	good	expert
26	Do you support your selling propositions with well thought out and compelling 'reasons to buy'?				

		poor	ok	good	expert
27	Do you have a structured approach…not leading with your best points…building up to your best points?				
28	Do you 'test the water' or 'trial close' during your presentation?				
29	Do you pass on useful tips, hints and techniques to sales people to help them 'sell through' all the products?				
30	Do you provide useful and relevant advice about displays and merchandising?				

Closing the sale

		poor	ok	good	expert
31	Do you recognise the 'signs' that it is time to stop presenting and start provoking a decision?				
32	Do you recognise 'buying signals' that are given out?				
33	Do you know a number of recognised 'closing techniques' to use at different times with different people?				
34	Do you directly/indirectly ask the customer if they would like to buy?				
35	Do you recommend 'add on' appropriate products or services to maximise the value of the sale?				

Continuous improvement

		poor	ok	good	expert
36	Do you take the time after a meeting to write up some useful notes?				
37	Do you take the time to reflect on the meeting and identify the things that *you did well?*				
38	Do you take the time to reflect on the meeting and identify the things that *did not go so well* – and understand why?				
39	Do you take the time to reflect on the meeting and identify the things that *you would do differently next time?*				
40	Do you learn from your meetings and customer interactions?				

Jonathan Frost